The Tranquil Garden

Country Living
GARDENER

The Tranquil Garden

Creating Peaceful Spaces Outdoors

text by Kay Fairfax
photography by Clive Nichols

Hearst Books
New York

Library of Congress Cataloging-in-Publication Data
Country living gardener the tranquil garden : creating peaceful spaces outdoors.
p.   cm.
Includes index.
ISBN 0-688-16407-2
1. Gardening.   2. Quietude.   I. Country living gardener
SB453.C75523   1999
712'.6--dc21   98-8318
CIP

Country Living Gardener
Editor Diana Gold Murphy
Editor-at-large Niña Williams
Horticulture editor Ruth Rogers Clausen
Features editor Rebecca Sawyer-Fay
Art director Jaye Medalia
Managing editor Lisa W. Quezada
Products editor Zazel Lovén

Produced by
Marshall Editions Ltd, The Orangery,
161 New Bond Street, London W1Y 9PA
Project editor Jane Chapman
Art editor Helen Spencer
Design assistance Philip Letsu
DTP editor Lesley Gilbert
Managing editor Clare Currie
Art director Sean Keogh
Production Nikki Ingram
Editorial coordinator Becca Clunes
Indexer Valerie Chandler
Horticultural advisor Tony Lord

Printed and bound in Italy by Chromolitho

FIRST EDITION
1 2 3 4 5 6 7 8 9 10

www.williammorrow.com

contents

INTRODUCTION 7

part one   part two   part three

Introduction

"The kiss of the sun for pardon,
The song of the birds for mirth,
One is nearer God's heart in a garden
Than anywhere else on earth."
DOROTHY FRANCES GURNE

Whether you live in the town or country, have a tiny patio, or are lucky enough to have acres of land, your garden should be a refuge from the stresses and strains of modern life, a place to observe the changing seasons and be at one with nature. *The Tranquil Garden* will inspire you to transform your outdoor space into a haven where you feel comfortable and rejuvenated and where all your senses are satisfied.

The opening section focuses on a range of garden-design styles to help you form a vision of the kind of garden that will bring you the most peace and pleasure. Perhaps your idea of a tranquil space is a wild garden bursting with a profusion of blooms – or you might prefer the

The scented golden yellow flowers of *Iris danfordiae* push bravely through a blanket of snow, reminding us that spring is just around the corner (right). An old, spreading apple tree throws wonderful dappled shade onto the lawn of a beautiful garden in the full bloom of summer (left).

balance and symmetry of a formal garden. For a low-maintenance option, look to the serenity of a Japanese garden, where elements such as water, gravel, stone, wood, and pebbles predominate. Alternatively, you could conjure up the essence of a Mediterranean or seaside garden. By introducing the elements that appeal to you – a water feature, a romantic arbor, or a handsome specimen tree – you will be able to create a unique space that reflects your own image of tranquility.

The following pages will encourage you to think about every aspect of your garden – from choosing planting schemes and hardscaping that create the most harmony to incorporating interesting vistas and

The eye-catching splendor of autumn is displayed in the brilliant red foliage of *Acer palmatum* 'Ôsakazuki' and the buttery yellow tints of *Acer × conspicuum* 'Silver Vein' (below).

focal points. You will see how elements such as color, pattern, texture, light, and shade can all enhance the visual balance of your garden; you'll also discover ways of ensuring that your garden blends comfortably with the house and surrounding landscape.

The final section concentrates on the functional and aesthetic details that can make a difference to the atmosphere in your garden. With a wealth of ideas and practical advice to help you choose such things as furniture, containers, water features, ornaments, and lighting, your tranquil garden will be a place that helps to refresh the spirit, relax the mind, and fill you with a sense of peace.

Winter in the vegetable garden has its own ethereal beauty. The terra-cotta pots bring hints of color to the muted tones of the still landscape (below).

part one

THE CHOICES

WHETHER YOU HAVE INHERITED AN already established garden or are beginning from scratch, you will need to spend some time assessing the space and deciding how it can be transformed into your vision of a peaceful paradise – a place where you can relax and leave the cares of the world behind you.

Walks in the country, days out at the beach, vacations overseas and at home, and visits to other people's gardens are all good sources of inspiration. Look around you and think about the things in nature that make you feel calm and relaxed, inspired or agitated. Would you prefer a garden that was predominantly green, with lots of trees and foliage plants, or would you feel more at ease surrounded by color? If you feel reenergized when you are near water, then consider introducing this element – in the form of a pond or a small fountain – into your yard. You might want to devote all or part of your garden to cultivating fruit and vegetables or perhaps you would like to create a sanctuary for wildlife.

Before you set about turning your dreams into reality, there are a few practical considerations to take into account. Decide how much time you can devote to gardening. If you have a high-maintenance garden, you might find that weekends do not give you enough time to stay on top of the work; and remember, even

Delphiniums, irises, tulips, and ranunculus bring
summer color to this informal garden. The conifer adds
depth and structure to the overall scene and helps to
incorporate the background trees into the garden.

container plants need regular watering. Do you plan to stay in your present home for the foreseeable future or do you intend to move after a few years? Do you want an instant garden or are you prepared to wait for trees and shrubs to become established? You might want to set aside an area for children or, at a later date, add a pond, a swimming pool, or even a greenhouse. Addressing these practicalities now will help you to avoid unnecessary stress and expense in the future and allow you to create a garden that is right for your lifestyle.

There is no one style of garden that is more conducive to peace and relaxation than another. It is simply a matter of personal taste. You might decide that a formal garden, with topiary, clipped hedges, and a parterre, is the epitome of tranquility, or you may prefer the seemingly untamed beauty of a wild garden. Perhaps you would like to create a romantic hideaway full of scented roses and a secluded arbor, or you might opt for the serene minimalism of a Japanese garden with a soothing water feature and restrained planting. The choice is yours, but remember that you don't have to import the look wholesale. A patio or terrace with a few pots and perhaps some windowboxes and shutters to decorate a wall might be enough to evoke the essence of a Mediterranean garden. Nor do you have to stick rigidly to one style. A modern sculpture could look stunning in a woodland setting, for instance, while an exotic plant could make a striking feature in a formal garden.

The following pages will give you a glimpse of some of the many styles you can choose and will help to guide you along the path toward creating a tranquil garden that is a unique expression of your tastes and aspirations.

A natural clump of the stately creamy white arum lily *Zantedeschia aethiopica* 'Crowborough' makes a stunning feature at the side of a pond or pool.

natural gardens

*"I have a garden of my own
But so with roses overgrown,
And lilies, that you would it guess
To be a little wilderness."*

ANDREW MARVELL

TO STEP INTO A NATURAL HAVEN burgeoning with plants that appear to have sprung up of their own accord and teeming with wildlife, a place where there is an apparent absence of rules, is perhaps the epitome of peaceful and relaxed gardening.

Regimentation plays no part in natural gardens. Serried ranks of municipal marigolds do not stand at attention in the parade ground of rectangular beds; spruced but scentless hybrid tea roses do not present arms in straight borders running the length of a precision-clipped perfect lawn. You tend not to see much bare dirt in natural gardens either, and few of the highly manipulated plantings of more formal gardens – bouquets of willow grafted to root stock and grown as standards, for example, or poles of twisted wisteria. The hanging basket – whether decked out in vibrant reds or in more restrained blues and yellows – is absent from the natural garden, as are geometric topiary figures and highly elaborate ornaments.

This does not mean, however, that a natural garden never has any statuary, that it never has straight lines, or a row of plants. A line of tepee stakes supporting the flowers of scarlet pole beans makes a charming feature, especially if you can pick up that color in rambling roses tumbling over a wall behind. A classical statue might look out over a seemingly natural fall of land toward a river. A modern bronze might be found rising from the rushes of a humble pond.

The colorful, daisylike flowers of asters are a magnet for butterflies (left). These informal steps, with ground-hugging plants wandering across and spilling over the edges, are at one with the landscape and help to create natural changes of level (right).

At first sight, the natural garden will appear to be a very simple, uncomplicated place. It will probably be overwhelmingly green, with lots of foliage and pretty trees, but its edges might also be full of shrubs and flowers, or, like a cottage garden, bursting with flowers and fruit and low plants, such as lady's mantle (*Alchemilla mollis*) or heathers such as *Erica cinerea* 'Pink Ice,' spilling over paths of mown grass, or flagstones or old brick. Because plants are encouraged to tumble over in this way, the natural garden is usually free of hard edges, rarely has gaps in flowerbeds, and almost always has charming little mounds of rock cress (*Aubrieta*) that have self-seeded in the cracks between the stones. A small stream or natural-looking pond will be edged with moisture-loving plants such as the yellow flag iris (*Iris pseudacorus*), ornamental rhubarb (*Rheum palmatum*), and the umbrella plant (*Darmera peltata*), all of which will help to attract a wide variety of wildlife to your garden.

The natural gardener prefers old-fashioned and informal flowers, as opposed to the highly cultivated fashion plates associated with the hothouse – columbines triumph over dahlias, buddleias over camellias. There is no place in the natural garden for the exquisite double varieties, arrived at by painstaking breeding and

Beds and borders spill over with a profusion of blooms in the natural garden. This raised bed has been painted to bring out the pink tones of the heucheras, diascias, nemesias, and ranunculus (left).

trialing, the "new" colors from the gene cupboard, or the dwarf versions of normally robust plants. Some people also take natural gardening to mean using only those plants that are indigenous. This is enthusiastically carried out in landscape gardening in parts of the United States and Germany where such plants are used in great drifts. Where this method is modified to include not just indigenous plants but also those species that thrive in the local climate and soil conditions of the area, it has the advantage of attracting back concomitant wildlife, especially birds. Perhaps the ideal solution is to combine natives with exotic plants in beds and borders.

While the natural garden is free of overelaboration, rigidity of shape, obsessive orderliness, and manicure, this does not mean that it is left completely to its own devices. The apparently artless profusion of nature – the eglantine rose (*Rosa rubiginosa*) rushing through an apple tree, skies of Virginia bluebells on the woodland floor – is in fact achieved by a respectful amount of management and control. For the rose to rush evenly, in the right direction, and as prolifically as possible, it must be pruned and trimmed and tied. If you want Virginia bluebells rather than brambles, you must be prepared to do the clearing first.

The most natural displays are created when plants are massed together. Here the majestic heads of *Tulipa* 'Princess Irene' rise above a sea of blue forget-me-nots (below) in a drift of glorious spring color.

formal gardens

THE CLASSIC ELEGANCE OF A FORMAL GARDEN, with its geometric plan of straight lines and rectangles, occasional perfect circles, and balanced curves, can have a calming effect on both the mind and eye. Symmetry, proportion, and balance are central, but this does not mean that a formal garden is difficult to achieve or requires a great expanse of land to be enjoyed. Nor does a formal approach exclude any decoration or elaboration. There may be architectural topiary and clipped hedges; edges of traditional species such as English yew (*Taxus baccata*) or boxwood (*Buxus sempervirens*); restrained rather than gaudy planting; and a focal point at the end of a long vista provided by classical urns, elegant statuary, a stone bench, or a symmetrical pond planted with water lilies.

Most formal gardens will have clipped trees or hedges, perfectly manicured lawns, and a minimum selection of plants. It is always wiser to plan this type of garden on paper first – whether starting from scratch or changing an existing one – so there is a disciplined framework before you add or change the plants. There is no room for waywardness with the hardscaping, lawns, or plants; there should be no unruly perennial borders filled with masses of riotous color; no paths going off at all angles or spilling over with plants; and no weeds in sight. There are no strict rules governing the species you use; but there should be a color theme, and plant combinations should be selected with care to maintain the symmetry of shape and color. You might choose an entire bed of lavender, say, or one filled with roses and edged with box or mondo grass (*Ophiopogon japonicus*).

One of the most popular elements of a formal garden is the parterre. This is an ornamental flowerbed that is divided into compartments to create a geometric pattern, and although it is traditionally associated with large gardens, the basic design can easily be adapted to suit a smaller area. The compartments are either raised or at ground level and are usually edged with box, while the plantings themselves tend to feature only one or two varieties that are repeated throughout the design. Lavender, santolina, irises, tulips, and roses are popular choices, but

An olive tree encircled by standard roses makes a stunning centerpiece at the intersection of lavender-lined gravel paths in this formal herb garden.

many others may be worthy of a place as long as the color combinations are not too strident. Even edible plants such as purple sage, parsley, or 'Little Gem' lettuces may be commandeered into service. A parterre often features a decorative centerpiece such as a sundial, an urn, a topiary statue, or a standard rose, fuchsia, gardenia, or daisy. The paths around and in between the parterre's compartments may be of grass, gravel, brick, sand, or colored stone chips.

Evergreen hedges of cypress, holly, boxwood, bay (*Laurus nobilis*), English yew (*Taxus baccata*), or privet can be used to create handsome living boundaries in the formal garden, and they also help to sustain interest during the winter months. Beech, although technically deciduous, retains its dead leaves throughout the winter and therefore makes an appealing yet changing screen throughout the year. Pleaching is an ancient technique whereby the lower branches of trees are removed and the lateral branches are entwined, giving the effect of a high hedge while leaving space underneath for a lawn or a planting. Trees suitable for this treatment include the linden (*Tilia platyphyllos*) and hornbeams (*Carpinus betulus*). A formal pleached or pollarded linden walk looks spectacular when used to line a driveway in a large garden.

A formal garden is not just about topiary, hedges, edges, and parterres. If you look at a Japanese garden, for instance, it appears very formal by the nature of its structure, design, and restrained use of plant material. The same can be said of many contemporary gardens, where a visual balance with the house is achieved with materials such as slate, tiles, wood, and concrete, and architectural plants are chosen for their shape and texture rather than for their showy blooms. Even the smallest of gardens can enjoy this approach. An orderly line of minimalist cuboid containers made from galvanized metal, say, rather than antique vases, planted with clipped evergreens such as sculptural domes of boxwood will help to bring an atmosphere of harmony and balance to a patio, roof garden, or courtyard.

A classic stone urn on a plinth makes an elegant focal point at the end of a path (right).

*"With statues on the terraces and peacocks strutting by;
But the glory of the garden lies in more than meets the eye."*
RUDYARD KIPLING

Symmetry and harmony prevail in this formal garden (above), where an immaculate herb parterre has repeat plantings in each compartment and a neat edging of clipped box. The limited palette of color makes a good foil for the more informal and exuberant border plantings. Evergreen trees and topiary sculptures bring exciting shapes and variations of height to the garden, whatever the season (right).

romantic gardens

*"The sweet forget-me-nots
That grow for happy lovers."*
ALFRED, LORD TENNYSON

IT WOULD BE DIFFICULT TO IMAGINE a more peaceful setting than a romantic garden. In spring it is alive with blossom and bulbs and the verve of fresh green shoots. Choose beguiling bulbs such as the azure-blue Siberian squill (*Scilla siberica*), the shy windflower (*Anemone blanda*), or the dancing creamy white flowers of the dog tooth violet, or fawn lily (*Erythronium californicum*).

In the transition between spring and summer, the romantic garden is bursting with the great clusters of peonies in its borders and clematis climbing up trellises and along pergolas. Then comes summer itself, with the soft overlay of roses on walls, generous borders of deep blue delphiniums, mauve bells of campanula, and white clouds of *Crambe cordifolia*. The night air is scented with stocks and nicotiana; the daytime is perfumed with lilies and roses. If the romantic garden in spring is a fresh, enthusiastic place, by summer it is wholly given over to the pleasures of the senses.

This is the wonderful thing about a romantic garden; it runs the gamut of sensibilities, from the innocence of virginal spring snowdrops to the voluptuousness of overblown blooms in high summer, from the fecundity of autumn harvests to the tragedy of incipient death as amber leaves zigzag in little gusts on their last flutter to the ground. Autumn and winter bring their own particular allure to the romantic garden. Rosy apples and glistening grapes encapsulate autumn's mellow fruitfulness, and a maple provides a final burst of fire, its tawny gold and bronze leaves creating a resplendent carpet on the ground. And don't be in a hurry to cut down the blackened stems and seed heads of the border; they provide food and cover for insects, birds, and animals when they need it most.

The severity of winter is a gift for the romantic garden. Plant hedges and edges and trees and shrubs with half an eye on how they will look laden with snow or bound in a thick frost. This means opting for variations in texture, using dark evergreens as a backdrop, looking for the most delicate of branches across which spiders may sling the tracery of their webs, and introducing contrasts – the paperbark maple *Acer griseum*, for example, produces peeling cinnamon-colored bark that gives warmth to the monotone tableau of snow.

No romantic garden would be complete without roses. A green clipped hedge forms a luxuriant backdrop to a cascading rose with an underplanting of *Allium rosenbachianum* (opposite). The essence of summer is encapsulated in the exquisite scented blooms of *Rosa* 'William Lobb' (above).

Autumn and winter can be the most romantic of seasons. A dusting of morning frost covers a carpet of beech leaves and brilliant red rosehips glisten under an icing of snow (above and opposite).

Generally, the less regimented the garden, the more romantic it will appear, but it is still possible to create a romantic garden with fairly formal hardscaping and softening it with informal planting. A man-made pond will never have its black plastic liner showing around the edge, for instance, and hard lines will be obscured by the foliage of plants such as rushes and flag irises. And of course, there will be lots of water lilies.

Scented plants such as sweet peas (*Lathyrus odoratus*), violets (*Viola odorata*), or daphne (*Daphne odora*) are an integral part of the romantic garden and will also serve to attract butterflies and bees. Use lavender and *Rosa rugosa* for hedging; create an intimate arched walkway smothered with a climbing rose such as *R.* 'Madame Alfred Carrière'; allow *R.* 'Albertine' to scramble over a fence; or grow a white *Jasminum officinale* against a wall so its delicious fragrance can waft near the house. There are countless ways of injecting evocative scents into your garden, but remember to keep the colors subtle so there are no harsh interruptions to disturb the mood.

Let structural features enhance the romantic atmosphere. A bower, nook, or arbor will provide a secluded spot for relaxation; so will a swing or hammock slung between a couple of old gnarled fruit trees. You might consider adding a bridge over a pond of water lilies to summon up a charming, small-scale version of Monet's garden at Giverny. Allow climbers such as clematis, laburnum, or wisteria to sprawl over a frame next to a wall and position a wooden or stone bench underneath. Encourage forget-me-nots and lady's mantle to self-seed between stone paths.

There is something quintessentially romantic about the garden of an old-fashioned property, whether it is a clapboard house in New England, an English thatched cottage, a crumbling farmhouse in Italy, or a rustic French barn. However, it is perfectly possible to create a romantic haven even in an urban setting. The terrace of a modern apartment, for example, could be transformed into an intimate space with a wooden deck, a café table, a couple of old steamer chairs, and masses of foliage plants spilling out from containers.

This romantic Japanese-style bridge conjures up the serenity of an Oriental garden and provides the perfect vantage point to enjoy the mesmerizing reflection of the early morning sun on the still surface of the water.

"I will hold my house in the high wood
Within a walk of the sea."
HILAIRE BELLOC

oceanside gardens

BEING CLOSE TO THE SIGHTS, SOUNDS, and smells of the sea inspires a feeling of peace and harmony with nature, and it is this that makes a coastal garden such a relaxing and uplifting place to be. Every sensory pleasure is enhanced, from feeling the sun on your back and the wind in your hair to listening to the waves lapping gently on the shore and watching the sun rise or set across the water.

One of the great advantages of gardens by the ocean is that they usually enjoy a more moderate temperature than those farther inland and often escape the worst effects of frost. There are also a number of drawbacks, with strong, salt-laden winds, blown sand, and poor, shallow soil being just some of the challenges facing the coastal gardener. These can all be overcome, however, if you do not try to compete with the natural landscape. Incorporate the sculptural qualities of rock outcrops into your site and continue the same natural hardscape elements in your garden design. Use stones, rocks, weathered wood, gravel, pebbles, driftwood, and shells.

If your site is steeply sloped, create natural-looking rock gardens integrated with a rugged path enticing you down to the water. Introduce salt-resistant, low-growing plants in natural clumps or drifts. Use as many indigenous species as possible, and stay away from too much harsh color and too many exotics. Choose scented plants such as lavender, rosemary, and Mexican orange (*Choisya ternata*), whose perfume will be carried on the wind. Ornamental grasses look magical waving in the breeze and provide year-round interest. Plants such as sea kale (*Crambe maritima*) and sea pink or thrift (*Armeria maritima*) have handsome foliage that will withstand desiccating winds. Many decorative plants thrive in the intense light, and pelargoniums, *Helianthemum* species, cascading geraniums, *Hydrangea macrophylla*, the silver-gray *Santolina chamaecyparissus*, brooms (*Cytisus* and *Genista*), and the daisy bush (*Olearia* species) are a small selection of those worth considering. Scatter seeds of the corn poppy *Papaver rhoeas* for a surprise in summer, and for a touch of formality grow espalier-trained apples or pears on a sheltered wall of the house.

Many exposed gardens require shelter from the buffeting winds. A living screen of trees or shrubs works best, and among those that do well are hollies, hawthorns, many of the pines, pittosporums, the holm oak (*Quercus ilex*), and *Escallonia* species.

Sea urchins nestle under the sculptural, sword-shaped leaves of an *Agave americana* 'Variegata' (above).

Maritime plants mingle with driftwood, rocks, railroad ties, and starfish in this coastal garden (left).

woodland gardens

A WORLD WITHOUT TREES WOULD BE A CONSIDERABLY DULLER, less harmonious place. Trees play a pivotal role in nature: they afford protection from sun, wind, and rain; they are essential to the survival of a vast array of flora and wildlife; and their leaves provide oxygen and nourish the soil when they fall. In addition to these life-giving properties, trees delight the eye and refresh the spirit whether they are in the town or country.

A woodland garden, whatever its size, allows you to enjoy these positive associations. However, the thought of planting and tending trees can strike fear into the heart of many gardeners. It is true that a badly chosen tree may grow too large for your garden, casting shade for most of the day and even causing some structural damage. But with a little foresight these problems can easily be avoided, and there is no reason why even a small garden can't include one or two eye-catching specimens.

Before you plant a tree, you need to have an idea of its ultimate height. As a general rule, try to plant it at least one-and-a-half times this distance from the house. You need to consider the amount of shade a tree will cast, not just on the house itself, but also on the rest of the yard. There must be enough light allowed to penetrate the crowns of the trees; otherwise, your garden will become a dank, sunless spot where the growth of other plants will be severely restricted. After all, there is not a great deal of life on a true forest floor. Choose deciduous trees, such as the Mount Etna broom (*Genista aetnensis*), that have an airy canopy that allows plenty of light to filter through.

Trees can be used in a multitude of ways. Where space allows, you can create your own version of a peaceful woodland with an underplanting of shade-tolerant bulbs or perennials, such as narcissus, trout lilies (*Erythronium*), or primroses; or plant a double line of trees to flank a path. In a smaller garden, introduce a single specimen,

"Loveliest of trees, the cherry now
Is hung with bloom along the bough,
And stands about the woodland ride
Wearing white for Eastertide."

A. E. HOUSMAN

The delicate leaves of a Japanese maple (*Acer palmatum*) turn dazzling shades in autumn. The carpet of fallen leaves is almost too beautiful to be walked on.

such as an ornamental cherry (*Prunus* species), as a striking focal point in a bed or the center of a lawn. Alternatively, use trees to make a stunning backdrop to a planting of ornamental shrubs such as hydrangeas and rhododendrons. Choose shrubs that will produce a display with more than one season of interest. *Fothergilla major*, for instance, produces sweetly fragrant flowers in spring and outstanding autumn foliage, and *Corylopsis pauciflora* carries pretty primrose-yellow flowers on bare stems before the leaves emerge. Trees can also be used as windbreaks and screens, and they will obscure an unsightly view. Remember, too, that a seat positioned under a tree makes an ideal place to sit and relax.

When you are planting one or two specimen trees, consider those that offer spectacular features, preferably for a long season of interest. Foliage is an important attribute, and maples such as *Acer japonicum* have handsome lobed leaves that produce exquisite autumn tints. Other desirable features to look for include bark, flowers, twigs, berries, and catkins. A crab apple (*Malus*) is a good choice since it combines a number of these qualities, including dazzling spring blossoms and spectacular fruits and foliage in autumn. Another candidate worthy of inclusion for its year-round appeal is *Amelanchier lamarckii*, which offers an arresting combination of white blossoms in spring and handsome scarlet leaves and dark red berries in autumn. The flowering dogwood (*Cornus florida*) is a hard-working small tree, combining red strawberrylike fruits, rich autumn color, and bark that flakes with age. The graceful *Betula utilis* var. *jacquemontii* is a birch with bark of the purest white and warm yellow autumn foliage.

Finally, consider how a tree's overall shape and habit will fit into your yard. You might opt for a tree with weeping branches, such as the silver-leaved pear (*Pyrus salicifolia* 'Pendula'), or for one that is upright and columnar, like the evergreen conifer *Juniperus communis* 'Hibernica.' Other trees may be round-headed or have spreading horizontal branches or contorted stems.

The shy, nodding white flowers of the Christmas rose (*Helleborus niger*) are a joy to behold when there is little else to cheer up the winter garden (below). Hellebores do well in shade or semishade in moist soil and are ideal for a woodland setting.

The spectacular *Cornus controversa* 'Variegata' is like a living sculpture, with its spreading horizontal branches resembling the tiers of a wedding cake (opposite). The dainty *Viola cornuta* spreads rapidly to form an enchanting purplish blue mat (above).

This tranquil woodland setting – at the Hannah Peschar Sculpture Garden in Surrey, England – cleverly combines the old with the new. Modern sculptures and an unusual bridge made from old oakwood planks are framed by the branches of a maple. An ancient stone seat makes the ideal place to sit and contemplate the view.

edible gardens

THE GARDENS OF PARADISE WERE FESTOONED with fruit trees and all manner of good things to eat. And, if you think about it, an Eden without food would be a contradiction in terms. After all, fruit, vegetables, and herbs do not just represent sustenance, they are also symbols of fecundity. So while a restful garden should please the eye, relax the mind, and refresh the spirit, it should also include all the physical delights – the tastes, textures, smells, sights, and satisfactions – of food. A garden where you can truly enjoy the fruits of your labor.

This is not to say that all edible gardens are peaceful or aesthetically pleasing, of course. You have only to think of commercial vegetable production, with tunnels for growing lettuce, for example, stretching in long rows as far as the eye can see. The tunnels cast an eerie light; the remorseless runs of infant salads have an unbroken visual monotony.

With its rather dull and utilitarian image, the vegetable plot is often banished to a remote corner of the yard, far away from the fireworks of the flowerbed. With a little planning and imagination, however, it is perfectly possible to create a garden that not only yields a harvest of homegrown produce, but is also a place of beauty and tranquility. Depending on the size of your garden and your requirements, you might decide to develop an old-fashioned

Tepees of scarlet runner beans inject a colorful note to the neatly laid out vegetable plot (left), while a handsome, fruit-laden lemon tree forms an eye-catching link between the house and garden (right).

kitchen garden, dedicated to production, with fig trees fan-trained against a wall, espaliered apples, and cordons of pears dividing neat furrows of potatoes, onions, and carrots, and with nets or cages protecting mounds of berries from marauding birds. At the other end of the scale, your edible garden may be a simple windowbox filled with aromatic herbs or a pot of blazing nasturtiums on the patio. In a town garden, you might consider the sophisticated addition of bronze fennel waving feathery wands behind the sculpted forms of elegant ivory lilies, or of luscious grapes lazing sensuously against a warm brick wall in the light of a September sun. You don't have to set up a market garden; just bring in some morsels of edibility.

If you do have a vegetable garden, try not to overplant your patch. It is more interesting – both visually and for the taste buds – to have a small number of different vegetables rather than monotonous lines of only one type. Introduce change by sowing different varieties of lettuce and growing vegetables that are attractive in their own right. Climbing beans, for example, are often grown as ornamental plants, and a mixture of red- and white-flowered varieties makes a splendid display. Fill any gaps in the bed with flowering ornamentals and edge with chives, parsley, or even dark blue trailing lobelia.

The European kitchen garden always had a section of cutting flowers for the house. But it is often the edible plants themselves that inject color and interest, transforming the garden into a feast for the eyes as well as the senses. Think of the exquisite blossoms on fruit trees, the brilliant flowers of pole beans, the blue stars of borage, and the red-purple globes of flowering chives.

An herb garden is an excellent way of combining the edible with the ornamental, and you don't need acres of land to produce a bountiful harvest of fresh herbs for the kitchen. Most herbs do well in containers, and apartment dwellers can make use of a windowsill. For a slightly larger, more formal planting, arrange your favorite herbs in a cartwheel formation, using either a real cartwheel or a facsimile constructed from bricks or wood. Choose decorative herbs such as rosemary, purple-leaved sage, golden marjoram, and fennel, and set off the display with colorful ornamentals such as pot marigolds or even a low-growing old shrub rose. The only stipulation is that the herbs should be easily accessible and, ideally, situated near to the kitchen.

An edible garden will offer visual delights throughout the year. In spring, apple trees are weighed down with frothy blossoms; the lustrous reds, blacks, greens, whites, and blues of berries spangle in the summer garden; the mellow days of autumn herald a rich harvest of pumpkins and squashes; and in winter a covering of glistening frost brings beauty to the herb garden.

A vegetable garden can offer a cornucopia of colors, shapes, and patterns, from a terra-cotta pot filled with fresh green parsley to the sunburst colors of pumpkins. In a highly imaginative modern setting of gravel and brick, the brilliant red stems and dark green leaves of ruby chard stand guard around a central pot of cabbages (opposite).

The luscious tomato 'Gardener's Delight' and the hot chile pepper 'Apache' add vibrant splashes of color to the vegetable garden (above and below).

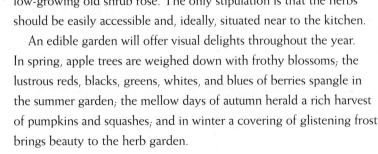

feng shui gardens

"This was among my prayers: a piece of land not so very large where a garden should be and a spring of ever-flowing water near the house, and a bit of woodland as well as these."

HORACE

FOR THOUSANDS OF YEARS THE CHINESE have used feng shui, the art of placement, to determine the location and alignment of their gardens, as well as the rocks, pools, and pavilions within them.

Literally meaning wind and water – the two forces that had the greatest impact on early Chinese civilization – feng shui is the art of maintaining a beneficial flow of life-giving energy, or chi. In the same way as a Chinese acupuncturist attributes health problems to a person's chi being blocked in a particular area of the body, so the energies of your house or garden may also be blocked.

A garden designed in accordance with the principles of feng shui will not follow a particular style in the same way as other gardens – a formal or a natural garden perhaps – will. To apply feng shui is more about manipulating your environment, both natural and man-made, to influence the way you feel in the best possible way.

You should be aware of what your needs are, what your problems are, and where you would like to make any changes and improvements. You might set up a garden as inspirational, for instance, if that is what is lacking. Or it might offer waves of calm and tranquility, if that is needed.

One popular misconception is that hard edges bring misfortune and curved ones don't. This is not necessarily the case, however. Rectangular lines in the approach to the garden or a square lawn surrounded by open borders denote clarity, space, and accessibility,

The visible part of a pond should always be constructed from natural materials such as stone or wood (opposite). A simple fountain with water trickling over an assortment of pebbles will bring harmonious sounds into even the smallest garden (left).

41

suggesting that there is nothing hidden in the lives of the people who live there. Conversely, a lot of curves may make a garden more interesting, but may also denote intrigue and secretiveness.

At a very simple level, feng shui can be seen as a metaphor for common sense and the principles of good design. If you plant a tree, for example, position it so that it will not put the rest of the garden in shade for most of the day. Inject more light by cutting back plants or introducing those with lighter or less dense foliage. Similarly, water in the garden is a good purveyor of chi, but it must be clean and free-flowing. Dirty, stagnant water is considered inauspicious – it is, after all, a breeding ground for disease – and should be purified with water plants and wildlife.

Harmony and balance are the watchwords of good feng shui in the garden. If you add a water feature to your garden, for instance, make sure it harmonizes with its surroundings. A pool near the house should be smaller than one situated farther away; otherwise, there is a risk that the chi will overwhelm the residents. In a similar vein, a brick wall or fence provides an effective barrier to structures such as drains or telephone poles, but you should counterbalance them with foliage plants and always make sure they blend in well with the rest of the landscape.

Trees, shrubs, and flowers – indeed anything living – all create good feng shui in the garden. Sweetly scented plants such as roses, lilies, and lavender are auspicious, as are climbers, particularly those with a good scent such as honeysuckle or wisteria; along with the pleasure of their fragrance, they can be used to conceal a bare expanse of wall and soften the hard corners of the house. Even in the smallest space, you can still enjoy the beneficial effects of plants with, say, a hanging basket by the door. The rounded shape of the basket allows chi to flow harmoniously.

The types of raw materials you choose can also have a dramatic effect on your garden's atmosphere. Suppose you wanted to introduce a focal point – perhaps an urn, sculpture, birdbath, or sundial. One of the first things you should consider is what it is made of. Stone, for example, is substantial and would have a solid, grounding effect; wood is generally lighter and considered to be uplifting, so this would have an inspirational effect; and metal suggests wealth, or a sense of completion in life.

Using colors such as vibrant reds is another good way to stimulate the flow of chi in your garden. Plants are an obvious choice, but you can also use seats, containers, and ornaments to inject sudden splashes of color. You should also aim to introduce soothing, harmonious sounds. Fountains, wind chimes, and delicate plants such as ornamental grasses that flutter in the wind are all most propitious.

Plants and running water are an excellent way to introduce movement into the garden. A stream should meander and flow in a gentle curve around the house.

mediterranean gardens

PROVENCE, IN THE SOUTH OF FRANCE, is famous as the center of the perfume industry, which is hardly surprising since the air itself in this part of the world is permeated with the delicious scent of lavender. In fact, you scarcely need a garden when all around you are hillsides of terraced vines and olives, blue fields of lavender stretching as far as the eye can see, wild aromatic herbs growing in abundance, and the Mediterranean Sea dancing blue and green under china skies. But of course there are gardens here, and if you could distill their essence, everyone would want a bottle.

The Mediterranean region offers a diversity of wonderful flora: magnificent firs and cedars, elegant pencil-slim cypresses, pines of every kind – stone, Corsican, beach, scrub – ancient olives, of course, and feathery tamarisk. If there were no flowers and only trees, you still could make a wonderful garden; but flowers do abound, and areas such as the Alpes Maritimes or the Sierras of Spain offer a rich cornucopia of wildflowers.

The choice of garden flowers is largely determined by the climate and terrain of the area. Generally speaking, the soil is rather poor, but it is good for geraniums cascading over terraces, rich cream and purple bougainvillea, and clouds of plumbago. One of the things that makes these flowers appear so full of vitality is the quality of light. Brilliant like a well-cut diamond, it gives an added luster to every flower, a sheen to every leaf.

To inject a little of this Mediterranean magic into your garden, start with the hardscaping and be brave. If you have stone walls, so much the better. If you don't feel they look particularly Mediterranean as they are, plaster them roughly and paint them in those terra-cotta colors often known as

Raised beds edged with old railroad ties overflow with a profusion of plants, some of which have been allowed to self-seed in the gravel path (opposite). The brilliant yellow heads of the sunflower (*Helianthus*) bring instant sunshine to any garden (above).

*"The woods, and desert caves,
With wild thyme and the gadding vine o'ergrown."*
JOHN MILTON

Tuscan or Etruscan. Alternatively, you could try blue. There is a turquoise used all over the Mediterranean that is half sea, half sky. It has to be said that it looks best in sunshine, however, so you may want to be more sparing of it than with other colors that have the advantage of warming up the surroundings. Remember, too, that fences, benches, gazebos, and containers can also be painted.

Be smarter with trees. If you live in a suitable climate, use the trees that grow all over the Mediterranean region, like the Aleppo pine (*Pinus halepensis*) or the Italian cypress (*Cupressus sempervirens*), sometimes known as the Mediterranean cypress. Other good pines include the Monterey pine (*Pinus radiata*), the stone, or umbrella, pine (*Pinus pinea*), and the scrub, or Virginia, pine (*Pinus virginiana*). The Italian cypress is only frost hardy, withstanding temperatures down to only 23°F (-5°C). For a fully hardy lookalike, choose conifers such as *Juniperus scopulorum* 'Skyrocket' or the dark green *Chamaecyparis lawsoniana* 'Kilmacurragh' or *C. l.* 'Wisselii,' which is bluish green and looks wonderful in spring when the tips of the branches are weighed down with tiny red flowers. For a hardy lookalike olive, try the sea buckthorn *Hippophaë rhamnoides*. It has similar long, silvery leaves, but instead of olives it bears masses of berries, resembling tiny balls of translucent fire, in autumn and winter.

Many plants associated with Mediterranean gardens tend not to be hardy. If your climate won't support them, you can grow them in terra-cotta pots and transfer them to the sunroom, conservatory, or greenhouse before the first frosts. Many plants, including oleander (*Nerium oleander*), daturas, and gardenias, do spectacularly well in containers, but you must be prepared to provide bigger and bigger pots and ultimately transport them in and out at appropriate times of the year. Hardier candidates for a Mediterranean-style garden include exotic-looking abutilons, showy sun roses, stunning blue gentians, brightly colored geraniums, and, of course, sweetly scented lavender.

The beautiful mellow tones of the stone make a splendid backdrop for a rustic window and need no further adornment than a few flowering pots (right). A classical stone statue tucked into a niche presides over a garden filled with vivid red bougainvillea, nicotiana, and *Cyperus papyrus* (opposite).

water gardens

OF ALL THE ELEMENTS THAT CAN BE USED to heighten a garden's restful qualities, it is perhaps water that offers the most scope. Bringing light, movement, and sound into the garden, water has a powerful effect on the senses and has the potential to calm, inspire, or excite. Small wonder then that rivers, streams, and fountains have epitomized the beauty and tranquility of gardens from earliest times.

The ideal for many of us would be a garden running down to a river or one that includes a natural pond or a little stream. Where this is not possible, however, we should look to man-made pools, ponds, and fountains to introduce the uplifting properties of water into our lives. If you are thinking of adding a pond, you may opt for one that will look "natural" and blend imperceptibly into the surroundings with flowers or foliage plants tumbling over the edges, or you may decide that a more ornamental, overtly artificial pond with a tiled or stoned border, for instance, would suit your style of garden better.

A rectangular pool or a rill (a straight, narrow, shallow channel of water) make elegantly restrained features in a formal setting. Another highly ornamental option is a shallow reflecting pool. A superb example can be found in Mrs. Whaley's garden

in Charleston, South Carolina – one of the most visited gardens of the eastern states – where there is a circular pool measuring only one inch deep and four feet in diameter. You can easily create your own version, but for a really dazzling effect, paint the base and sides of a very shallow pool black and position it so it will catch the reflection of an overhanging tree or shrub.

Mirror plantings of bamboo, astilbes, and hostas dress the sides of this elegant pool. The impressive leaves of a fatsia hang over the wall behind and irises emerge swordlike out of the water (right). The green tones of the leaves and moss enhance the warm terra-cotta tiles of this unusual fountain and rill (left).

"In the deserts of the heart
Let the healing fountain start."
W.H. AUDEN

While the formal rectangular pool does not necessarily need much planting or ornamentation to dress it, and the shallow circular pool can be left unadorned or looks magical at night simply lit from underneath, the "natural" pond will need some planting. To maintain the ecological balance of your pond, you should aim to introduce plants at different levels. Submerged plants such as curled pondweed (*Potamogeton crispus*) are important, especially if you wish to keep fish, as they oxygenate the water and prevent it from becoming stagnant. There are also floating plants, including the majestic water lilies, and a galaxy of plants that will thrive at the water's edge. Choose the moisture-loving goatsbeard (*Aruncus*), with its feathery plumes of cream flowers, or the more delicate astilbes, such as the white *A.* 'Deutschland', whose finely cut, fresh green leaves make a good background for candelabra primulas with their tiered circlets of pinks and mauves. *Ranunculus*, a member of the buttercup family, includes cultivars ranging in color from ivory to brass, and its cousin, the common marsh marigold or kingcup (*Caltha palustris*), looks scintillating when the golden flowers are caught by the sun's reflection on the water. Another choice for moist ground is *Clintonia andrewsiana*, with lily-of-the-valley leaves and dark rose to violet balls at the end of its wavy stem.

Hostas, with their exquisite foliage, are also suitable for waterside planting, but while they love damp and perform well in shade, they hate to be waterlogged. It has to be said, however, that many hostas, especially the variegated ones, often look too cultivated in a natural setting. Ferns, with their delicate, feathery foliage, might be a more appropriate choice, while sedges such as *Carex elata* 'Aurea,' with its arching, golden, grasslike leaves, can be grown in shallow water or damp soil. *Glyceria maxima* var. *variegata* is another impressive marginal with gracefully arching, strap-shaped leaves that are striped cream and soft green. Among the most delicate of all waterside flowers are angel's fishing rods (*Dierama*), whose frilly, rosy bells are suspended from an almost invisible arching stem.

Massed plantings of bog-loving plants flank a gently flowing stream. Red and pink rhododendrons and a Japanese maple inject splashes of color (right).

Some of the irises, including the yellow flag iris (*Iris pseudacorus*) and the magnificent *I. laevigata*, with soft mauve-blue flowers, are wonderful plants for moist soil or shallow water. If frost is not a problem, the Louisiana irises, native to the swamps of the southern states, run a virtual rainbow of colors; while the distinctive creamy white flowers and arrow-shaped leaves of the stately arum lily (*Zantedeschia aethiopica*) look wonderfully exotic at the edge of a pond.

Even the smallest of gardens can benefit from the soothing qualities of a water feature or two. A simple wall-mounted fountain will introduce a note of serenity to a noisy in-town garden, especially if the water trickles gently onto a mound of pebbles surrounded by pots of ferns and other foliage plants. And tubs, troughs, or sinks planted with *Acorus gramineus* 'Variegatus' or a miniature water lily such as *Nymphaea tetragona* will enliven even the tiniest patio. For further information on water features, see pages 182–83.

The charming rose-pink flowers of the water lily *Nymphaea* 'Fabiola' look romantic floating on a sunny pool. The leaves help to shade the surface of the water and make perfect landing pontoons for dragonflies (above).

wild gardens

THERE CAN BE FEW MORE PLEASURABLE EXPERIENCES than lying in the sunshine of early summer in a meadow of native wildflowers, and it is perfectly possible to recreate an approximation of this idyll in your own backyard. A wild garden should not be confused with a wildflower garden, however. A wild garden usually means a garden that doesn't look as if it has been cultivated at all (though, of course, it has), and is simply bursting with prolific plants which nature has provided (though, of course, it has done nothing of the sort). You will see nothing as obvious as beds and borders in a wild garden, no shrub will appear to have been trimmed or pruned, and all staking will be surreptitious. Nevertheless, it will look wonderful. And the point about a wild garden is that you can incorporate cultivated plants if you want, while a wildflower garden means just what it says.

You can create a wild garden in almost any situation. Even a small town garden can be transformed into a green oasis, if not overnight, then at least within a couple of years. Make your boundaries high – if necessary, mount trellis on top of a wooden fence – and plant fast-growing, self-clinging evergreen climbers such as the semievergreen chocolate vine (*Akebia quinata*), with vanilla-scented, dark dusty rose flowers. For a warm garden, choose the frost-tender *Sollya heterophylla*, whose nodding bells of sky-blue flowers appear from spring to autumn. For an enchanting all-blue scene, throw in masses of grape hyacinths (*Muscari*) or add clumps of the early-flowering *Iris reticulata*.

For a fully hardy evergreen climber, try *Euonymus fortunei*: *E. f.* 'Coloratus' turns purplish in winter and 'Silver Queen' is variegated green and silver all year-round. Honeysuckle and ivy are two nother hardy stalwarts for the wild garden, and the evergreen confederate jasmine (*Trachelospermum jasminoides*), with its sprays of sweetly scented white flowers, looks wonderful against a brick wall. As for ivies, try combining a mixture of cultivars. *Hedera helix* 'Green Ripple,' for instance, has small, finely cut bright green leaves; *H. h.* 'Glacier' has silvery gray and green leaves edged in white; and those of *H. colchica* are dark green. Use these as a backdrop to a display of pale, looming foxgloves for an irresistible combination.

Avoid introducing very bright flowers or plants with gold variegation into the wild garden. The former tend to look too overtly exotic, and the latter somewhat over-cultivated, even if they're not. Flowers that are white or blue or a subdued purple or muddy rose are more appropriate choices. And whatever the size of your

Plants such as *Ajuga reptans* 'Catlin's Giant,' *Geum* 'Borisii,' and *Corydalis flexuosa* 'Père David' nestle effortlessly in a garden that appears to have sprung up as nature intended. Natural materials have been incorporated to reinforce the wild beauty, with a path of bark and a step made from an old railroad tie leading the eye onto the roughly mown grass path beyond.

The banks of a cascading stream are dotted with clumps of daffodils and *Anemone blanda* (opposite). A wild summer garden bursts with a profusion of plants, including sea buckthorn *Hippophaë rhamnoides*, blue *Campanula rotundifolia*, red valerian, *Linaria vulgaris*, *Veronica spicata*, and wild thyme (above).

"I like to see flowers growing, but when they are gathered they cease to please."

CHARLOTTE BRONTË

garden, you will create a wild effect more readily with very tall plants. In some parts of your garden, you should not be able to see over the top of them. Thistlelike plants fulfill all these criteria admirably. The imperial-looking cardoons, for example, were much prized by the Victorians and have impressive spikes of purple flowers towering over arcs of pointed silvery leaves. In front of these grow the pale mauve spheres of the globe thistle (*Echinops bannaticus*), with its thin, deeply cut leaves, and sea hollies, whose cone-shaped heads are framed by jagged lavender ruffs. Among the loveliest of these are *Eryngium alpinum*, in a tutu of feathery spines, and the statuesque *E. giganteum*, with silvery blue flower heads. Their ability to attract butterflies and bees further secures their place in the wild garden. Other nectar-rich plants to consider include asters, lavender, sedums, and butterfly bush (*Buddleia davidii*). Grow clumps of these in a sunny, sheltered spot.

In bigger gardens you can afford to spread out. Spires of white rosebay (*Epilobium angustifolium* 'Album') and sprays of the white, fragrant tobacco plant (*Nicotiana sylvestris*) look magical in front of a group of European white birch trees. Gardens in warmer climates will support the evocative combination of tree ferns (*Dicksonia antarctica*), with their crowns of unfurling fronds swooping over paths of naturalized arum lilies (*Zantedeschia aethiopica*) winding in a bridal train underneath.

japanese gardens

"Clear and deep-brimming is the pond,
Fresh is the garden with opening flowers,
Frolicking birds skim the waves, then scatter,
Pleasure boats wander among the isles."

ISHIKAWA SEKUSAKA

THE TRANQUILITY OF JAPANESE GARDENS has proved an enduring source of fascination in the West. We are inspired by their calm minimalism and at the same time captivated by the scarlet bridges, lanterns, and teahouses. Japanese gardens were built for contemplation, meditation, and peace; and by borrowing certain elements of their design, you can introduce some of these positive associations into your own garden. Indeed, their basic simplicity and restraint provide the perfect antidote to the stresses and strains of modern life.

One of the great distinctions between Japanese gardens and those of the West is that Japanese gardens are more built than planted. The emphasis is on structure rather than flora, and more importance is placed on permanence than on ephemeral beauty, with an intense aesthetic appreciation of natural materials and native plants. The inherent qualities of natural materials – the texture of stone, the grain and color of wood – are central to the garden's atmosphere. Every stone, pebble, drop of water, and grain of sand has significance and is steeped in tradition and symbolism.

Japanese gardening is characterized by the imposition of control refined to the ultimate degree. Even in gardens specifically designed as a homage to nature, nothing is allowed to grow wild. Instead, the *stroll*, or landscape gardens, are designed to show on a small scale the way nature appears on a grand scale. The placing of a tree and rocks around a pond, for example, might mimic the view of a certain lake and mountain. Another important element of Japanese gardens is the principle of *shakkei*, or borrowed landscape. This simply means incorporating the areas beyond the boundaries of the garden, such as water, trees, hills, or mountains, and not blocking them out of the vista, a concept that is applied to many styles of gardens today.

When planning a Japanese garden, the important thing is to keep it simple and uncluttered. The basic components are moss instead of grass if possible, water, white gravel or sand, and wood. Rocks are also integral elements, chosen for their color, structure, and texture. Plants are valued for their form and foliage, rather than for

A simple bamboo water spout surrounded by a planting of hostas and smooth stones makes a tranquil water feature (right), while the spectacular foliage of a Japanese maple provides the perfect backdrop for a classic Japanese-style bridge (opposite).

their flowers. Worthy of inclusion is a Japanese maple (*Acer palmatum*) or a dogwood, with their flaming autumn foliage contrasting brilliantly with the cool expanse of surrounding white gravel. Hostas, bamboos, pittosporums, azaleas, and the Japanese wisteria (*Wisteria floribunda*) are also appropriate. Evergreens such as pines, cedars, and junipers are widely used, and a covering of snow on their upper branches is regarded as a seasonal flowering.

The foundation of the garden is made up of gravel or sand, which is raked and kept in immaculate condition. This is surrounded by moss and a few carefully chosen, strategically placed rocks. There should, ideally, be a water feature, such as a small linear pool with fish or a planting of irises. Where there is no water, however, the sand or gravel symbolizes water, and the way in which it is raked represents the flow. Man-made construction elements such as paths and bridges form part of the landscape of the Japanese garden; and in addition to their functional role, they serve as a reminder that humans, too, are part of nature.

Remember that you don't need to import this look completely. It is not about cramming your garden with rocks, stones, and fountains at every turn, but choosing the elements that are appropriate for you in order to capture an essence of the serenity and peace of Japanese gardens.

A drinking vessel rests on a natural rock surrounded by raked gravel, with smooth stones taking the place of plants. The low bamboo fence separates the inner garden from the outer plantings of moss and bamboo (opposite). A wooden bridge traversing water is a common feature of Japanese gardens. Here the light green leaves of an *Acer palmatum* var. *dissectum* and the yellow flowers of *Caltha palustris* 'Flore Pleno' introduce splashes of color (right).

The handsome timber
pavilion – reached by
stepping stones over a
large pebble pool – is
the perfect place to
contemplate the soothing
sights and sounds of the
tea garden. A traditional
stone lantern sits on
a base of large stones
in the foreground, while
a stunning purple-leaved
Japanese maple and
waterfall can be seen
in the background.

exotic gardens

LUSH GREEN FOLIAGE PLANTS WITH GIGANTIC, exaggerated leaves and stunning, vibrantly colored flowers with a strong heady perfume all growing in a hot and steamy environment – these are the things that people usually associate with an exotic garden. But it is not essential to have the climate or rainfall of an equatorial rain forest in order to enjoy a little taste of tropical paradise. The word "exotic" is also used, after all, to denote something that is strikingly, intriguingly different. In the same way that the flora of a foreign country captivates the visitor – the eucalyptus trees of Australia, the sculptural cacti of South America, or the swaying palm trees of the Caribbean – so it is possible to introduce this element of the unusual into your own garden.

The key ingredients are color, shape, and texture. Use green as the predominant shade to provide a lush, tranquil background and against this add visual surprises. Fuchsias, such as the vigorous and hardy 'Mrs. Popple,' and the stunning pinks, mauves, and blues of hydrangeas all make powerful statements. Choose climbers such as bougainvilleas, the passionflower (*Passiflora caerulea*), *Rhodochiton atrosanguineus*, and the trumpet vine (*Campsis radicans*) for their distinctive, showy flowers. A wall of espalier-trained fruit trees dripping with luscious figs, pears, or rosy red apples provides a feast for the senses.

The art of companion planting, combining, perhaps, vegetables and flowers, offers an effective way of introducing an exotic twist into the garden. In France, where this type of planting has long been practiced, a typical scheme could include standard roses, carrots, and masses of nasturtiums mixed with

Plants such as yuccas, *Cordyline australis*, and *Agave americana* offer lush, architectural foliage and can be grown in pots (left). With its exquisite flowers, the bird of paradise (*Strelitzia reginae*) brings an instant hint of tropical color (above).

"I will make a palace fit for you and me
Of green days in forests and blue days at sea."
ROBERT LOUIS STEVENSON

the dark green leaves and brilliant red stalks of ruby chard and the feathery spikes of fennel. There will be tepees of pole beans and sweet peas, red and yellow tomatoes trained on stakes, and the entire display will be edged with parsley. You can create your own variations on this theme, but remember that the secret is to incorporate contrasts of shape, texture, and color.

Enlist the services of architectural plants to bring weird and wonderful shapes into your garden. The spiky, palmlike leaves of New Zealand flax (*Phormium tenax*), *Cordyline australis*, or *Yucca filamentosa* all make exotic statements and look sensational when teamed with the feathery fronds of ferns such as *Athyrium filix-femina*. Euphorbias, cardoons, and sea hollies are also prized for their shape and stature. For a dramatic display of bulbs consider a dense planting of parrot tulips or *Fritillaria imperialis*, and for a touch of the unusual try training gourds over an arch or pergola instead of the usual vine or creeper.

To create a mini jungle on your doorstep, start with a framework of green plants such as the statuesque tree fern *Dicksonia antarctica*. Clumps of architectural bamboos, with their long thin leaves, make wonderful focal points and in the proper climate, where there is room, team these with the great fat umbrellas of *Gunnera manicata*. For a blast of color grow fiery red-hot pokers or exotic cannas. Where hardiness is a problem, you can grow plants in an assortment of pots and tubs and transfer them indoors when the temperature drops.

Along with the planting, you should also try to incorporate accessories that will enhance the exotic atmosphere and help to give the garden balance and cohesion. For hard surfaces choose colorful tiles, terra-cotta pavers, gravel, pebbles, or stained wood. Furnish with wicker tables and chairs; use large terra-cotta pots or oil jars for dimension; and add wall-mounted or freestanding sculptures to create focal points. You could even create your own version of a tropical swamp with a pond brimming with water lilies, water irises, and sedges and surrounded with lush foliage plants.

The kaffir lily (*Schizostylis coccinea*) is native to southern Africa, where it is usually found growing by streams. Given a moist, well-drained soil, the spikes of lustrous pinkish red flowers and bright green sword-shaped leaves produce an alluring display in late summer and autumn (above).

The stunning cobalt blue used on the walls and around the pool conjures up the feeling of an exotic Moroccan-style garden. Contrasting yellow pots planted with cacti and a magnificent bougainvillea add to the effect (opposite).

stage set

TO CREATE A PLACE WITH DREAMLIKE QUALITIES, where there is a total sublimation of the senses, a place that conjures up a sense of drama but one that is tranquil at the same time, is not as difficult as it sounds if you think of your garden as a stage set. It can be large and as extravagant as your pocket is deep or cozy and intimate as a small terrace, balcony, or courtyard. Whatever size your stage may be, the same principles of design should apply. It must be in proportion and there should be careful attention to detail. So let your imagination run wild and add a touch of theater to your garden.

A stage setting in a large garden can be created from living sculptures such as hedges or topiary. Trees and shrubs – boxwood (*Buxus sempervirens*) and English yew (*Taxus baccata*) are the usual choices – may be clipped into intriguing shapes, such as animals, birds, or even a complete chess set. Grandiose architectural sculptures can take years of patient clipping to perfect, but the same effect can be achieved on a small scale by using ivy trained on wire frames or boxwood clipped into small balls and pyramids. Being evergreen, ivy and boxwood add interest to the winter garden, and look especially beautiful with a covering of snow.

Use part or all of your garden to re-create the magic of another country. Transport yourself to a corner of Italy, for instance, by laying old stone and adding urns planted with small trees such as an olive, lemon, bay, or a dwarf cypress. Fill tubs with cascading geraniums and train a flowering creeper such as bougainvillea up a wall or over a trellis. Add a small statue, an umbrella, and some café-style furniture. Alternatively, you could conjure up the essence of France by paving with

A stunning trompe l'oeil painted in an old stone doorway and plantings of deep purple irises, pink alliums, and a citrus tree help to bring the warmth of Provence to this cobbled terrace (left).

The *tour de force* of this modern garden is a stained-glass panel set in solid frames. Ornamental grasses and *Verbena bonariensis* help to soften the hard surfaces (above).

"In his blue gardens, men and girls came and went like moths among the whisperings and the champagne and the stars."

F. SCOTT FITZGERALD

warm clay tiles, whitewashing outside walls, and adding shutters. Fill terra-cotta pots with rosemary, lavender, and masses of nasturtiums, and allow grapevines to scramble up pergolas and trellises.

Introduce a taste of the East Coast with clapboard or wooden decking, gravel, and a few large rocks. Intersperse some majestic grasses and relax in director's chairs. Or to evoke the serenity of an Eastern garden, start with wood, brick, or concrete tiles. Add a small symmetrical pond or rill, and fill it with fish and a few water irises. You could also construct a gravel or pebble garden with pots of bamboo or a Japanese maple (*Acer palmatum*). Another source of inspiration could be an English garden full of flowers, lawns, boxwood hedges, statues, and stone paths. Add pots and urns overflowing with spring bulbs, perennial borders bursting with voluptuous peonies, and a hammock between two old fruit trees to provide a perfect place to relax.

part two

THE PERSPECTIVES

A GARDEN SHOULD BE A HAVEN OF relaxation and enjoyment, a place where you go to escape the stresses and strains of everyday life and where all the senses – sight, smell, sound, touch, and even taste – are satisfied. To create such an outdoor retreat, whether you favor the untamed beauty of a natural garden or the serene minimalism of a Japanese-style garden, you will need to make sure that the sum of its parts adds up to a balanced, cohesive whole. All the elements that go into making a garden – color, shade, light, planting, hard structures, and ornaments – should blend comfortably together. And there should be visual harmony between the house, the garden, and the landscape beyond.

Whether your garden is large or small, in the city or the country, it is important that it blends well with the surrounding environment. If you are lucky enough to overlook an attractive view, don't blot it out but aim to incorporate it into your garden. If there is nothing to borrow or if you look out onto an eyesore, compensate by creating a substitute landscape, with a handsome boundary, perhaps, or a screen of trees. Similarly, the house itself should form a visual link with the garden. Adding an outdoor room such as a terrace, a patio, or a simple pergola is one way to blur the boundaries between the two.

Mirror plantings in restrained greens, yellows, and whites add to the overall visual unity of the setting and help to link the neoclassical temple with the pool.

Before you rush off to the local garden center, you need to have an idea about which plants will flourish in your garden. Your choice will be determined to a large extent by environmental factors such as rainfall, temperature, and the type of soil in your area, but you also need to take into consideration such things as the position of your site and the amount of shade or sunlight it receives. Do you live on an exposed hillside that is buffeted by strong winds or are you surrounded on all sides by tall buildings? Coastal gardens will need to withstand salt-laden winds, while in towns and cities pollution from traffic might be a problem. Once you have a clearer idea about your garden's microclimate, you can then start to think about the plants you would like to include and what colors, shapes, and textures most appeal to you.

Think, too, about the way hardscaping can be incorporated to improve the overall balance and harmony of your garden. You may want to include a path to link the house with the garden or perhaps create an outdoor eating area. A water feature, in the shape of a small formal pool dotted with water lilies or a romantic pond with plants tumbling over the sides will enhance the atmosphere of tranquility in any garden. Statues, birdbaths, topiary figures, and seats all make stunning focal points and can help to draw the eye to a particular part of the garden.

Finally, try to remember that gardening should be a pleasure, not a chore. Have fun experimenting with different planting ideas and learn by your mistakes. A few failures along the way will only serve to heighten your sense of achievement when those bulbs you planted reward you with a magnificent spring display.

Flanked by a double perennial border, a long grass path leads to a striking focal point of clipped boxleaf honeysuckle. The date palm (*Phoenix roebelenii*) in the center is grown in a container so it can be wintered indoors.

garden and landscape

THE SCENERY THAT LIES BEYOND YOUR GARDEN'S boundary can have a powerful impact on the overall visual composition. Integrating the surrounding, or borrowed, landscape with the cultivated garden has been practiced for centuries in the East. So, if you do overlook a harmonious scene, try to incorporate it into the garden's design. There might be a distant view of rolling green hills with cattle or sheep grazing, a mesmerizing glimpse of the sea, or an alluring tapestry of fields, hedges, and stone walls. Mountains, trees, lakes, streams, even a spectacular sunset can all become part of a stunning backdrop to a garden.

If you are lucky enough to have a natural landscape that abuts the garden, the most important consideration is to create a gentle transition between the two elements so that the borrowed landscape effectively becomes part of the private garden. Clever use of softscaping or planting will allow you to form this link without harsh interruptions. A semiwild area of rough, unmown grass between a lawn and the edge of a woodland, for instance, will help to give the impression of continuity. Similarly, creating different levels – perhaps a gently sloping bank planted with shrubs and trees of differing heights receding into the distance – will help to blur the demarcation between a cultivated garden and the natural landscape.

An uplifting view should be seen and enjoyed from the garden, so make sure your boundaries don't obscure it. Deciduous trees will help to give a greater sense of space and openness than a dense planting of tall evergreens. If you have a high, thick hedge, consider adding an arch or gate to provide a tantalizing suggestion of the vista beyond, and choose open fencing wherever possible. Opt for sympathetic planting that echoes the terrain of the surrounding landscape, be it rolling and verdant, rugged and mountainous, or coastal. Introducing native species, rather than too many jarring exotics, will also help to bring a sense of balance and harmony.

While a rural landscape may offer many jewels to the gardener, in towns and cities where there is little or no natural scenery, incorporating the borrowed landscape can prove much more of a challenge. Perhaps you look out on an unprepossessing view

This small stream forms a natural transition between the paved area and the grassy landscape beyond. A seat has been positioned to take full advantage of the splendid weeping willow.

"All gardening is landscape-painting."
ALEXANDER POPE

of a neighbor's fence or a bare brick wall dotted with drainpipes and ventilators, or overlook an inauspicious urban vista of rooftops and chimneys. Look beyond the immediate boundaries of your garden, however, and you might be surprised to discover an interesting feature that will enhance the unity and tranquility of your garden. A group of trees in a nearby park, a towering church spire, a distant view of a river, or the elegant façade of a nearby building can all be used as interesting focal points. And where there is nothing scenic on the horizon, create your own point of interest with a living screen such as a hedge, a row of evergreen trees, or even a line of container-grown shrubs. Introduce an eye-catching specimen such as *Acer palmatum*, with its blazing autumn foliage, or *Prunus* 'Spire,' which carries clouds of pale pink flowers in spring, followed by a stunning display of autumn tints.

To divert attention from an ugly view and to add height to an urban garden, mount sturdy trellis on a fence, and train ivies such as *Hedera helix* 'Glacier' or an ornamental grapevine (*Vitis vinifera* 'Purpurea') against it. Enliven a bare wall or fence with a stunning, self-clinging Boston ivy (*Parthenocissus tricuspidata*), whose maplelike

The natural landscape beyond a garden's boundary can offer seasonal variations of interest. Bare wintry branches peep over the snowcapped hedge of this formal garden (opposite above), while a background of green foliage plants makes a wonderful foil for a summer display of towering mauve alliums, white geraniums, and blue polemoniums (opposite below).

A bank of roughly mown grass rolls gently down to the edge of a stream, with the impressive leaves and stately flower spire of an ornamental rhubarb (*Rheum palmatum* 'Atrosanguineum') growing on the bankside. A wooden bridge links the garden with the wild area beyond (right).

leaves are flaming shades of crimson and scarlet in autumn. Alternatively, paint the wall a vibrant blue or a more mellow terra-cotta and add wall-mounted containers spilling over with geraniums and petunias. Transform an eyesore such as an old shed or garage into an attractive feature with a camouflage of clematis or honeysuckle.

A roof garden or balcony can offer the perfect vantage point from which to view a dramatic cityscape. Create a tranquil haven with masses of green foliage plants and pots of aromatic herbs and scented shrubs, clipped boxwood hedging, or topiary. Erect a pergolalike structure using overhead trellis to provide some dappled shade, and allow pot-grown climbers such as *Jasminum officinale* or *Wisteria floribunda* 'Alba' to scramble over it. Install a table and chairs and retreat there at the end of the day to enjoy the magic of the city lights.

With their spectacular white bark and early autumn color, these birch trees (*Betula utilis* var. *jacquemontii* 'Jermyns') form a natural gateway from the private garden to the countryside beyond (left). A grass pathway winds round a vibrant bed of pink and red azaleas into the woodland (opposite).

house and garden

"Just now the lilac is in bloom,
All before my little room."
RUPERT BROOKE

THE INHERENT CHARM OF MANY OLD RURAL properties – from a clapboard farmhouse in Connecticut to an English stone cottage – lies in the fact that they merge so comfortably and imperceptibly with their surroundings. They appear so peaceful and welcoming because they are built on a sympathetic scale using local materials, with colors and textures that are in keeping with the landscape. By contrast, many modern homes do not share this affinity with their surroundings. The yard often appears to have been added on almost as an afterthought, with the result that there is little cohesion between the two areas. With a little planning and foresight, however, there are many ways to improve this situation and make sure the house and garden coexist in harmony.

You should think of your yard as an extension of your home. It is essentially another room, and as much care and attention to detail should go into its decoration as to any other room in the house. The garden should also sit comfortably with the surrounding landscape, so decide which features you would like to incorporate. Perhaps there is a distant view of a river or the ocean, or, if your garden is in town, a dramatic cityscape or a handsome specimen tree in a neighboring garden. Before you make any changes, it is always a good idea to look at other gardens in your area and decide which look most at ease with their surroundings.

It is important that the garden offers a pleasing prospect from inside the house. Look carefully at the view from different levels and angles, and at different times of the day – from an upstairs window, through a doorway, or from a roof terrace or balcony. Does the garden enhance the room and blend harmoniously with the landscape beyond? Does the vista calm or irritate you? There should also be some visual interaction between the decor of the interior and the planting scheme outside. It might be rather jarring, for example, to move from a red room into a garden full of hot oranges. A garden that has a predominantly green-and-white scheme might be a more restful option. It is also worth carrying out a similar inspection on the house, this time looking into the interior from the garden.

A kitchen window looks out onto a veritable jungle of lush exotics, including bamboo and eucalyptus (opposite), while an open door invites you to step through the vine-clad arch into the sunny courtyard (left).

Framed by hanging vines and accented with blue glass, this enchanting view looks up a formal brick path lined with pots of cyclamen, lilies, and clipped topiary (opposite). The informal paved area with plantings on either side links the summerhouse with the immaculate lawn (below left). An archway smothered in the creamy yellow fragrant flowers of *Lonicera etrusca* eases the transition from the house to the walled Victorian kitchen garden with its rows of spinach, lettuce, and cauliflower (below right).

One effective way of blurring the boundaries between house and garden is to add an intermediate structure such as a porch to link the two elements. In areas with a hot climate a porch is an important addition to the house, serving as an extra living room or dining area. A pergola with space for a table and chairs underneath is another choice for relaxed alfresco living and can improve the entire ambience of the house, especially if you train climbers to scramble over the structure. Good candidates for this would be the white-flowered potato vine (*Solanum jasminoides*) or *Wisteria sinensis*, which carries abundant fragrant, blue-violet flowers.

Where space is limited, make a feature of a door by erecting a simple arch. With heavenly scented climbing roses cascading over it and pots of aromatic herbs on either side, you will create a welcoming entrance that can be enjoyed from inside and out. A small paved area dotted with pots and tubs spilling over with seasonal plantings will also help to ease the transition from house to garden. This is also the

ideal spot to introduce one or two exotic specimens – perhaps a stately pineapple flower (*Eucomis comosa*) – that can easily be brought indoors for the winter if necessary. If you have a stone path leading into the yard, allow plants to self-seed in the cracks to soften the hard edges, and consider adding a long archway, covered with sweet peas, laburnum, or *Rhodochiton atrosanguineus*, to form an enchanting corridor linking the house with the garden.

The architect Frank Lloyd Wright once observed that a "physician can bury his mistakes, but the architect can only advise his client to plant vines." The gardener should take comfort from these words; for there is indeed much that can be done to

A doorway dressed with painted shutters and flanked with tropical plants and a pair of ornaments leads into this exotic coastal garden (right).

disguise defects on the exterior of a house and make it more sympathetic with the garden. Enliven a drab wall with self-clinging climbers such as the stunning ivy *Hedera colchica* 'Dentata Variegata,' the crimson glory vine (*Vitis coignetiae*), which has spectacular autumn tints, or a Virginia creeper (*Parthenocissus quinquefolia*), whose leaves turn a beautiful shade of crimson in autumn. There are also a number of shrubs that can be trained flat against an uninspiring wall to inject color and interest. Try ceanothus, fuchsia, *Cotoneaster horizontalis*, or fremontodendron, which bears masses of sunny yellow flowers. Transform an unappealing but necessary garden structure such as a garage or shed into an appealing feature with a twining clematis or a rambling rose. And remember that windowboxes filled with a profusion of colorful geraniums, petunias, or begonias will not only help to dress up the outside of the house, making it more convivial to look at from the garden, but can also help to improve the vista from inside.

An open garden room looks out onto a lush tropical scene, with an enticing glimpse of the ocean beyond (below).

composition

A TRULY TRANQUIL AND RELAXING GARDEN, no matter where it is situated or what its style or size, is one where all the various elements within it blend comfortably together to form a balanced and cohesive whole. The composition of a garden is the big picture and encompasses such things as the natural landscape beyond the boundaries, the design, the planting, the hardscape, and the ornamentation. With a little planning, time, and effort, it is possible to unite all of these individual components to create a garden that is both aesthetically pleasing to look at and a joy to be in.

Begin by assessing the hard structures in your garden and think about any basic construction work that may need to be carried out to improve the overall layout. Your first consideration should be the house itself (see also pages 78–83). Unless you are building a new home from scratch, there is little that can be done to change the basic design, but there are steps you can take to make sure the house looks more at

For a wonderfully soothing effect, try combining contrasting shades of green. In this potager edged with box, culinary herbs such as feathery fennel and peppermint make a decorative and verdant display (left). A border featuring *Lavandula angustifolia* 'Hidcote,' eryngiums, and ferns presents a delightful composition of colors, heights, shapes, and textures (opposite).

ease with its surroundings. Outside rooms such as a terrace, a conservatory, a pergola, or a patio, or structures such as a path or simple archway, can all help to create a gentle transition between the house and garden.

Next, look at any existing structures such as fences or sheds and decide which ones you are happy with and which ones should be altered or even replaced. You may want to construct a new wall or path, lay a lawn, or perhaps introduce a pool. You may even wish to remove trees or large shrubs to accommodate a new flowerbed or vegetable patch.

When the basic framework is in place, you can then begin to decorate your garden. The planting scheme you choose will play a central role in cementing the overall cohesion of your garden. To a large extent, your choice will be dictated by the style of garden you wish to create as well as by environmental factors such as climate or soil, but the plants you include should always be an expression of your own tastes and preferences. Some people's idea of a haven might be a garden

Framed by a grapevine, this wall-mounted wooden trough makes a spectacular show (below). The plantings include yellow pansies, mimulus, *Lysimachia nummularia* 'Aurea,' and *Tiarella cordifolia*.

overflowing with flowers in a riot of colors, while for others a minimalist garden with very restrained planting would be the epitome of tranquility.

Whatever style you choose, there are many ways in which plants can be used to enhance the visual composition of your garden. Try to include some specimens that will offer a long season of interest – *Amelanchier lamarckii*, for instance, boasts white spring blossom and stunning autumn foliage – and remember to include some evergreens for year-round appeal. You can also use plants to create changes of level: a judicious planting of different-sized shrubs and trees, say, will add dimension to a flat site. Enlist climbers to conceal an unprepossessing wall or to mask a jarring eyesore.

Finally, position garden ornaments where they will be seen to the best effect and not be lost among other distractions, and choose garden furniture that is in keeping with the setting and situate it in a sheltered spot that commands a good view.

Rising above a mound of variegated hostas and the wooly gray leaves of *Stachys byzantina,* the pure white flowers of *Tulipa* 'Mount Tacoma' glisten in the morning sun in this exquisite study in green and white (right).

color

THERE ARE VERY FEW THINGS IN LIFE that have a more powerful impact on the emotions than color, and nowhere is this response more profound than in the garden. Color is a very personal subject, and in order to create a planting plan that is right for you, it is worth looking at the way different colors work together. White light is composed of a spectrum of colors – red, orange, yellow, green, blue, indigo, and violet – and when these are arranged in circular form to produce what is known as a color wheel, you will see that the colors next to each other, yellow and green for example, are harmonious, while those on opposite sides of the wheel, such as blue and orange, are complementary. In gardening terms this means that a bed of harmonious colors will be subtle and soothing, while one full of purples and yellows, for example, will create a striking, stimulating effect.

Remember, too, that color can be used to cool a place down or warm it up, and can also help to change the visual dimension of a garden. Cool colors tend to recede, so a garden filled with shades of silver, blue, and mauve will help to create an impression of space, while warm colors such as yellow, orange, and red advance, making the garden feel closer and more intimate. By grading the colors – starting with the hottest reds at the front and working to the coolest shades at the back – you can create an illusion of length. Similarly, a far boundary wall painted in one of the cooler colors will help to make the garden appear longer.

Bearing deep yellow flowers with a dark orange throat, the scented *Crocus chrysanthus* 'Gipsy Girl' makes a joyful sight in spring (below).

Inject splashes of warmth into the garden with the intense orange-red papery lanterns of *Physalis alkekengi* var. *franchetii*, the shocking-pink trumpets of *Mirabilis jalapa*, or the sunshine yellow of a rudbeckia (opposite).

*"When daisies pied and violets blue
And lady-smocks all silver-white
And cuckoo-buds of yellow hue
Do paint the meadows with delight."*
WILLIAM SHAKESPEARE

The brilliant red leaves of staghorn sumac dangle from their stems in autumn (above).

The famous English gardener Gertrude Jekyll was a great advocate of gentle gradations of color in the garden. For a perennial border she would begin with a planting of vibrant reds and oranges in the center and then grade the colors down at each side, ending with cool blues, to give a unified and restful display.

Whether you decide to combine a number of colors – either in a profusion of different hues or in more harmonious gradations – or prefer the single-color approach, with a predominance of reds, whites, or blues, you will need to use plenty of green foliage plants to set off the display. Evergreens make an excellent green canvas against which to add splashes of color and will help to give a visual balance to any scheme. The refreshing greens of ferns, grasses, and herbs also make excellent foils.

Try to include a selection of plants that will offer exciting seasonal variations of color. In spring, bright blue grape hyacinths, the scarlet flowers of the flowering quince *Chaenomeles* × *superba* 'Texas Scarlet,' the lilac clusters of *Syringa vulgaris*, and the strident yellows of forsythia provide a joyous burst of color. Offset the frothy pink of cherry blossoms with the fragrant, starry white flowers of *Magnolia stellata* and pink and white tulips, and frame the display with the white-margined leaves of a hosta or the silvery leaves of a santolina.

The summer garden is ablaze with a rich palette of color, with something to suit every taste from gaudy pelargoniums to the restrained whites and pinks of roses. Autumn is resplendent with fiery reds and oranges and more mellow browns and yellows. There are late-flowering dahlias and chrysanthemums in tones of cream and russet, and the bright orange, papery baubles of the Chinese lantern (*Physalis alkekengi*) smother the ground. Winter, too, brings its own brand of colorful magic to the garden with the graceful, dangling, gray-green catkins of *Garrya elliptica*, the spectacular bare red stems of a red-stem dogwood (*Cornus alba*), the cheerful yellow of a winter jasmine (*Jasminum nudiflorum*), and the exquisite flowers of winter aconite.

From the delicate pinks and whites of the orchid *Phalaenopsis* and the soothing blue-green of the red cabbage 'Rodeo' to the vibrant reds of the tomato 'Gardener's Delight' and the bright yellow of the mountain ash berries – the garden offers a spectrum of wonderful color (opposite).

Green is perhaps the most important color at the gardener's disposal. Here clipped evergreen hedges and long grass paths provide a perfect backdrop for the mirror plantings of the perennial borders, with their splashes of white red, pink, and yellow.

vistas and focal points

"A garden without its statue is like a sentence without its verb."

JOSEPH W. BEACH

IF YOU CONSIDER THE INTERIOR OF YOUR HOME, there are a number of vistas and focal points that help to connect the various areas and bring visual interest to the space. A hall or corridor leading you from one room to another, stairs to take you to a different level, windows that draw you forward to look at the view, and a doorway inviting you to enter a room where your eyes alight on a focal point such as a fireplace. Just as these elements help to unite the house, so it is in the garden, where such things as paths, steps, and arches help to lead your eye to a particular focus or to a distant view.

Every garden, even the smallest terrace or patio, should have a center of attraction, some object or plant, perhaps, that is in the direct line of vision and leads your eye straight to it rather than to the surrounding area. As long as your focal point is in proportion to the rest of the garden, it can be as extravagant as a folly or ruin or as simple as a sundial or birdbath. Eye-catching planting schemes could include an immaculate parterre, an elegant weeping tree, or a romantic pond full of water lilies; on a smaller scale, a single topiary sculpture, an architectural yucca, or an antique vase planted with a standard rose or spilling over with the abundant white flowers of a marguerite daisy all make visually arresting statements. Areas set aside in the garden

Peeping out from a profusion of yellow Welsh poppies (*Meconopsis cambrica*), this whimsical, weathered stone man makes a charming, informal focal point at the base of a tree (left). For a more formal approach, an ornate stone urn mounted on a brick plinth is framed by a beech archway flanked by a pair of wooden barrels planted with hydrangeas (opposite).

for rest and repose – an arbor, pergola, or a simple stone bench under a tree, for instance, or perhaps a medieval grass seat encircling a flowering tree or a weathered wooden bench in front of a hedge – all make welcoming points of interest, as does an old wooden gate with an archway covered in fragrant climbing roses or an iron gate that allows you a glimpse of the view beyond.

In smaller town gardens, wall-mounted sculptures or water features can serve as interesting focal points to cheer up a bare wall or to deflect attention from an uninspiring view. A trompe l'oeil – featuring a painting of a dream garden, perhaps, or an imitation window made from mirror and lattice – creates a wonderful illusion of space and adds atmosphere to a drab wall. A wisteria or an espalier-trained fruit tree such as a fig (*Ficus carica*) also looks magnificent against a sunny wall.

In the same way as a path or driveway at the front of the house should steer you in the right direction to the door, and not take a confusing, circuitous route via the trash cans or garage, so you will create a harmonious vista in the garden if there is something that will guide you either physically or visually to the point of interest. If you have a shady retreat in the garden, a gazebo or an arbor perhaps, there should be a walkway formed from a row of trees, a line of hedges, a pergola, or a simple path leading you toward it.

The magical silvery foliage of *Pyrus salicifolia* 'Pendula' looks striking at the intersection of gravel paths (opposite). Focal points can range from a single eye-catching specimen, such as *Allium hollandicum* (right) with its stately purplish pink spheres, to a captivating trompe l'oeil painted in a stone doorway (far right).

In a small garden, having too many focal points can be distracting, but in a larger space you might want to create a series of vistas. In order to avoid confusion, however, there should be directional guides – a wooden gate or archway, a bridge across a stream, the curve of a flowerbed – indicating which way to proceed. Introducing a change of level, with a gently sloping path, say, or a flight of stone steps with wandering plants self-seeding in the cracks, will also help to draw the eye from one part of the garden to another without interrupting its visual unity.

If you are lucky enough to overlook an area of natural scenery, try to incorporate it into your garden to create another stunning vista and to give your garden an extra dimension. Make sure the view is not blocked by too many evergreen trees and create a gap in a high hedge to provide a glimpse of the ocean or hills beyond.

Finally, it is important to make sure the view can be enjoyed from inside the house as well as from the garden. To look out of the window onto a tree in blossom, a verdant lawn, or a courtyard filled with pots of herbs refreshes the spirits, but when there is nothing more to recommend the prospect than a neighbor's garage or a busy road, you can manufacture your own miniature vista with a colorful windowbox or even a vase of flowers.

A modern stone sculpture sits serenely on a plain timber plinth in a woodland setting (opposite). In a large garden, an old summerhouse is a welcoming sight at the end of a path lined with pink and white Japanese azaleas (right). On a smaller scale, a wicker bee skep makes an arresting feature surrounded by mint (above), while a blue ceramic pot filled with red nasturtiums catches the eye on a patio (top).

frames

THE CORRECT FRAME AND MAT WILL ENHANCE and complement a picture or painting, not overwhelm it or distract the onlooker from the main point of interest. For a bold, geometric subject, which is full of depth and color, a neutral mat and simple, unobtrusive frame may be all that is required, while a paler, more delicate image might need a stronger border to give it definition and to prevent it from fading into the background. The same principles also apply to the garden, where such things as a line of trees, a gap in a hedge, doors, and arches form the frames for a series of tableaux – from a distant view of rolling hills to a colorful flowerbed.

A low garden gate in a wall or fence might look rather uninspiring, but add a simple arch over the top and cover it with fragrant roses and it becomes a romantic feature in its own right, drawing your eye to the view beyond. In the same way, a door can be transformed with a fresh coat of paint and the addition of an archway festooned with clematis or wisteria. Flank the door with a pair of matching pots

An arched Gothic-style gateway opens onto a charming paved cottage garden where a life-size statue stands in quiet repose (opposite). In a more formal setting, architectural clipped hedges make a good backdrop for the pool planted with grasses and pink irises, and help to frame the avenue of limes beyond the stone steps (right).

THE TRANQUIL GARDEN

planted with scented, flowering shrubs, herbs, or topiary figures and add hanging baskets cascading with colorful summer blooms. A door framed this way will look as wonderful from inside the house as it will when viewed from outside.

Windowboxes, climbers, and even an espaliered fruit tree can be used to dress the front of the house and frame the windows. They also help to frame the view when you are looking out of a window into the yard. Make a feature of a wall-mounted fountain or sculpture by framing it with climbers or an attractive planting at the base.

Paths are a good way to frame areas of the yard such as a lawn, and they look marvelous when they are bordered on both sides with a narrow bed of santolina, catnip (*Nepeta × faassenii*), or box. Try reversing the effect so the path – with plants such as *Alchemilla mollis* and forget-me-nots self-seeding in the cracks – becomes the

Varying shades of green create a natural framework for the white flowers of *Lunaria annua* 'Alba Variegata' and *Tulipa* 'White Triumphator' (left).

canvas and is framed by the lawn. Garden beds also create more impact when they are framed by an edging of some kind. A low border of clipped boxwood or santolina, for instance, will add definition to a rose garden.

A wall, hedge, or spreading tree will make a good backdrop for a stone bench or timber seat. A hedge might be thick enough to cut out a space for a seat or else you can erect a pergola with roses or laburnum scrambling over it. A natural-looking pool or pond should have its edges framed with marginals such as the flowering rush (*Butomus umbellatus*) or *Iris laevigata*. A flight of stone steps can also be softened by crevice-dwellers such as helianthemums. Steps will also ease the transition from one level to another. Another way to frame the steps would be to position a matching pair of pots or urns on each side at the point of ascent or descent.

A natural timber pergola with an overhead canopy of grapevine creates a perfect frame for viewing this lush, tranquil garden (right).

balance

DESIGNING AND PLANTING A GARDEN so that it represents a unified, harmonious whole that is pleasing to the eye, where there is a sense of balance and proportion, requires the same level of planning and attention to detail that goes into organizing the interior of your home. In a comfortable, welcoming living room, for instance, there is enough space left between the furniture to allow ease of movement. Tables and chairs are not all piled into one corner, leaving the rest of the room empty; paintings do not adorn every available inch of wall space. There is also a balance of layers: a tall bookshelf is not positioned in front of a small table; a cupboard does not obliterate the view from a window.

Forming masses and voids this way is also central to creating a cohesive and relaxing garden, whatever its style or size. Think of the lawn or any open areas as the floor, and trees, shrubs, hedges, and structural features as the furniture. There should be an even balance between the two to create harmony. Too much of one or the other will result in the whole being out of proportion.

When looking through the lens of a camera to take a photograph, the object is to fill the frame. You move a little to take in more or to leave something out if it does not appear balanced. Try looking at your garden this way before you make any drastic changes. This will show you where there are too many gaps, or voids, or if there are too many similar-shaped plants all clumped together. You should also make sure there is some link between the garden and the house. If there is a great void between them, perhaps you should consider adding a feature such as a pergola or a patio, a planting of shrubs, or even a group of containers to ease the transition.

A bed with plants of all the same height and shape can look rather monotonous, so creating different layers is a good way to add interest and impose a sense of balance.

A group of plants of different shapes, colors, and sizes creates a harmonious balance between the solid architecture of the house and the rest of the garden (below).

A brick path is bordered by mirror plantings of lavender with alternate rows of red and green lettuce. Tepee stakes swathed in sweet peas add interesting variations of height (right).

Planting taller species at the back with medium-height ones in the middle and smaller or horizontal varieties in front also adds depth to the garden. If you have two beds flanking a path, use mirror plantings on each side to give a sense of balance. You could intersperse a low bed of lavender with tepees of sweet peas or nasturtiums to give variations of height.

You can also introduce interesting changes of level with steps, low walls, paths, a hedge, or perhaps a bush of Mexican orange (*Choisya ternata*). A tall statue or specimen tree will make an exciting focal point in a larger garden, but in a courtyard or small yard, a large olive jar or terra-cotta pot with low plantings or a variety of smaller containers at the base will create a pleasing balance of shapes and heights.

Color plays a central role in creating a balanced garden. The most harmonious schemes are usually achieved when color is used in drifts – in a perennial border, for instance – rather than as a punctuation mark dotted around here and there. Texture and shape can also have a profound impact on the garden's overall balance. The spiky leaves of an iris, for instance, will sit comfortably with the soft, rounded leaves of *Alchemilla mollis* and the feathery foliage of love-in-a-mist (*Nigella damascena*).

A flight of mellow steps constructed from old railroad ties with gravel treads introduces a gentle change of level. The large terra-cotta pots planted with osteospermums help to create a visual balance (opposite). With sunny clumps of yellow *Iris pseudacorus* and mounds of spiky and feathery foliage at the water's edge, this pond blends effortlessly with the surrounding landscape (right).

In a spectacular
woodland setting and
on a carpet of natural
rough grass stands the
dramatic and perfectly
balanced slate sculpture
"Spires," by Herta Keller.

109

boundaries

"Before I built a wall I'd ask to know
What I was walling in or walling out,
And to whom I was like to give offence."
ROBERT FROST

AVAILABLE IN MANY DIFFERENT SHAPES AND SIZES, the boundaries of a garden fulfill a variety of functions. They may be situated on the perimeter of the property where they afford at least a measure of privacy and shelter for both you and your plants, or they can be used in a more central location to divide the garden into different areas. Some boundaries are purely functional, others make highly decorative additions to the garden. Fences and walls can be constructed from natural or man-made materials, or for a living boundary choose hedges and trees.

In rural areas, boundaries are frequently erected in order to keep livestock either in or out and also to act as windbreaks. Many old country gardens have two or even three levels of boundary. The outer one is often left open to the view and is made of wire or wooden fencing, or it is a natural barrier created by a ditch. Closer in are the hedges, perhaps an orchard, tall trees, and low stone walls. And still closer to the house there might be a high stone wall enclosing a garden of flowers, herbs, and vegetables. In urban areas, the main purpose of an outer boundary is to provide protection and privacy.

Wherever you live, it is important to choose a boundary that suits your requirements. You should also try to use materials that are in keeping with the surrounding landscape and are appropriate for the style of your home – a stone wall for a country cottage, perhaps, brick or wood for a town garden, and concrete blocks

A gate, painted apple-white and set in an evergreen hedge, creates a charming inner boundary, drawing you inexorably to the delights of the garden and to the outer high, brick boundary wall and wooden gate beyond (left). Another good choice for an inner boundary is this low, white picket fence (opposite). It makes an attractive foil for the colorful profusion of summer flowers and allows the plantings on the other side to be seen through the gaps.

to echo the design of a modern building. Before you build a wall or erect a fence or hedge, it is a good idea to check local regulations on the style and height permitted, especially if you live in a heritage or landmarked area.

Pliable and permeable and offering good protection against the wind, living fences satisfy many of the criteria of a good boundary. With their inherent softness and beauty, they can also make attractive features in their own right, and they provide a haven for wildlife. Evergreens such as English yew (*Taxus baccata*) or holly (*Ilex aquifolium*) make strong, dense barriers and provide year-round privacy; for a decorative inner hedge, choose a low-growing lavender or a taller *Rosa rugosa*.

Fences are inexpensive and easy to erect, but they can look rather stark and uninviting. To alleviate the monotony and to add extra height, attach a trellis to the top of an existing fence and cover it with climbers, or paint the fence dark green to blend in with any trees in the background. Old stone or brick walls have their own charm and may need no embellishment, but a blank concrete wall can be softened with a climbing rose or transformed with whitewash. A fence made from hazel, willow, or brushwood is a natural-looking alternative to a paneled version, while one made from bamboo would be perfect for a Japanese-style garden. For a cottage garden choose a picket-fence style.

Inner boundaries, such as paths, gates, steps, pergolas, archways, beds, and even ponds, can all help divide the garden into separate compartments.

The painted trellis constructed in front of a solid timber fence is perfect for training climbers such as this grapevine (above).

A natural-looking fence of logs screens an old weathered seat (right), while a high boundary of trellis with a yellow fremontodendron trained against it makes a good backdrop for the blue border (opposite).

An old stone wall covered with the spectacular cascading blue-violet racemes of *Wisteria sinensis* is an irresistible sight.

114

light

IT IS A CURIOUS THING, BUT WHILE the most experienced and knowledgeable gardeners will take account of almost everything when selecting plants – soil acidity, rate of growth, spread, habit, color, texture – the thing that often gets left out of the equation is the one that makes all the difference – natural light.

Changing from season to season and at different times of the day, light is not only essential in greater or lesser quantities for optimum growth of plants, but it is also central to a garden's beauty and atmosphere. Think about the delightful dappled effect that is created on the ground when sunlight filters through a canopy of trees or the dancing reflection of the sun on a pond. If you are considering planting an almond tree, for instance, try to position it so the pale, exquisite blossoms catch the morning sun. Similarly, the sun's rays will add fire to the scarlet autumn tints of a paperbark maple (*Acer griseum*) and will illuminate the spectacular polished mahogany bark of *Prunus serrula* to dramatic effect. Sometimes you discover that something you have planted has grown tall enough to be backlit by the sun and has been transfigured by this gift of light. A Matilija poppy (*Romneya coulteri*), for instance,

Here are two dramatic examples of light in a garden: an explosion of white as the sun strikes up the blossoms of a flowering Japanese cherry (left), and the mass plantings of *Hesperis matronalis* var. *albiflora* and the silver foliage of *Stachys byzantina* (below).

looks wonderfully ethereal when it is shot through with the silk of the early evening sun. Its white papery petals look as thin as gossamer, and its yellow stamens become a gilded crown.

In the same way that windows allow light into your home, you can take steps to manipulate the levels of natural light in your garden. Thin out any dense trees to allow shafts of light through their canopy. If you have a high, thick hedge, consider adding an arch or gate to open up the space, and leave gaps in the top of a pergola to create contrasts of light and shade.

With all its subtle nuances, natural light is one of the most useful tools at a gardener's disposal, adding interest and helping to lift the spirits. However, the constant glare of full sun is not necessarily conducive to peace and relaxation, and gardens that are bathed in sunlight for most of the day should have at least one shady retreat. A wisteria scrambling overhead on a trellis will help to diffuse some of the heat and light on a sunny patio. You might clothe the wall of a house with Boston ivy (*Parthenocissus tricuspidata*), green all spring and summer, which will take some of the heat out of the wall and make it cooler to look at. You might plant a spreading deciduous tree on a corner to shade the terrace and part of the house, not in deep gloom, but in dappled light; in autumn, the fingers of sunlight that filter through the tree's dying leaves will paint the ivy's auburn tints with flecks of gold.

The pretty magenta petals of *Geranium psilostemon* take on a translucent quality when they are illuminated by the sun (below).

Golden evening light casts soft shadows across the green lawn and picks out the 'Iceberg' roses, delphiniums, and penstemons of the luxuriantly planted perennial border (right).

*"For, where the welcome sun came through,
A delicate, rising green was new."*

JOHN WYNN

Remember, too, that plants themselves can be used to great advantage to cast an illusion of light. The horizontal branches of the kousa dogwood (*Cornus kousa*) glisten with white blossoms in early summer, while the yellow-green bare stems of *Cornus stolonifera* 'Flaviramea' make a dazzling winter display. Plants with white or silver foliage, such as the stunning weeping pear (*Pyrus salicifolia* 'Pendula'), with its white and felted leaves and creamy spring blossoms, or *Populus alba*, whose leaves literally shimmer in the wind, also help to radiate light in the garden. Enliven a gloomy spot with an unexpected clump of luminous white tulips or the dangling white bells of Solomon's seal *Polygonatum × hybridum*. Continue the optical illusion with towering spikes of white foxgloves (*Digitalis purpurea* 'Alba'). The bright yellow flowers of the winter jasmine (*Jasminum nudiflorum*) will bring a golden hue to the garden even on the darkest of days. A white seat, creamy sandstone, gravel, whitewashed walls, a stone statue, or a wall-mounted mirror to catch the reflection of a pond will also help to inject light into a garden.

A sundial surrounded by the tall spires of pink and white foxgloves (*Digitalis purpurea* Foxy Hybrids) is perfectly positioned to catch the late afternoon sun (left). The delicate papery lanterns of *Physalis alkekengi* var. *franchetii* bring a luminous beauty to the garden (right).

shade

WHILE A GARDEN THAT HAS GOOD LEVELS of light is usually regarded as a blessing, for many gardeners shade is seen as something of an obstacle. "Nothing will grow there, it is far too shady" is a common lament, but, in fact, all gardens need some shade, even if it is provided by a single tree or shrub, or a simple awning over the patio. In gardens in the Southern Hemisphere, shade is of paramount importance and is considered an advantage, not a disadvantage. Many plants – and humans, too – benefit from some dappled shade for all or part of the day. Moreover, a garden with good contrasts of light and shade will be more interesting and atmospheric than one that is bathed in constant sun. So, instead of thinking of a shady area as difficult, regard it as a positive attribute, a place where you can relax and be comfortable and where you can grow plants for their delights, such as dramatic foliage and interesting shapes and textures.

The degree of shade – from lightly dappled to dark and gloomy – will dictate the choice of plants that can be grown in a particular area. If your garden is overshadowed by tall, thick trees, you can thin out the canopy to let filtered light through. And remember that deciduous trees will let in more light than evergreens. Many plants grow happily on forest and woodland floors, but the soil under large trees is usually dry and hard, so any species planted under them need to have a shallow root system to compete for moisture and nutrients. One way of dealing with this situation is to improve the soil conditions with compost, manure, or other organic substances. Remember, this area needs to be kept well watered also.

Damp shade is generally easier to contend with, and there are many species that thrive under these conditions. Many ferns, for instance, require damp, shady situations to survive, as does the giant lily (*Cardiocrinum giganteum*) and *Clivia miniata*.

Wonderful contrasts of light and shade help to make this courtyard garden such a cool, refreshing place. The lush green plantings and the moss-covered rocks around the pool and fountain enhance the tranquil atmosphere (right). These whimsical ceramic planters surrounded by bright green ferns will enliven any shady corner (left).

"As the shadows fell, the stars came out."

DEREK JARMAN

Before planting, study your garden to see where and at what time of day shade appears. Camellias and the tree peony (*Paeonia suffruticosa*), for instance, need morning shade, while hydrangeas prefer shade in the afternoon. Rhododendrons, including azaleas, prefer semishade, or at least dappled light, and are ideal for planting under taller deciduous trees. As they both have very shallow roots, they need to be kept well watered and not allowed to dry out. Masses of *Cyclamen hederifolium* in autumn or a covering of creeping dogwood (*Cornus canadensis*) in late spring or early summer also make a splendid display in a woodland setting. Fuchsia hybrids need a semishaded position, and violets prefer light shade. For a shady spot choose hostas, with their wonderful variety of colors, shape, and foliage, or a Lenten rose (*Helleborus orientalis*), which combines nodding flowers in late winter and early spring with handsome evergreen foliage.

The exotic red blooms of *Canna* 'Le Roi Humbert' teamed with the imposing leaves of a banana (*Ensete ventricosum*) will bring a touch of tropical excitement to the garden (right). An overhead canopy of *Catalpa bignonioides* provides some shade for a stone pot of *Lamium galeobdolon* 'Hermann's Pride' (opposite below), while a pergola with laburnum trained over it makes a comfortable place to sit away from the full glare of the sun (opposite above).

The dappled shade from deciduous trees makes the ideal setting for many enchanting planting plans. An oak or birch wood carpeted with Virginia bluebells, lily of the valley, wild garlic (*Allium triquetrum*), snowdrops, and native ferns is an uplifting sight in spring. It is the contrast of light, shade, and color that makes these natural settings so perfect and peaceful, and you should try to incorporate these elements into your garden whenever possible. If you are erecting a long archway or tunnel, for example, make sure there are gaps left in the overhead section to allow the light to filter through, creating a dappled effect on the ground. If you are thinking of adding a pond, try to position it so it will receive some dappled light.

Tall buildings and high, thick trees or hedges can cast a permanent shadow, shrouding the garden in shade for most of the day. With judicious planting, however, it is possible to transform a dull space into a tranquil and verdant haven that is brimming with interesting shapes, patterns, and textures, and full of soothing

shades of green. Choose lush, shade-tolerant foliage plants such as hostas, ferns, and bamboos, and inject splashes of light with variegated plants such as *Aucuba japonica* 'Variegata,' whose handsome, glossy leaves are spotted with gold. For architectural value, add a striking *Rodgersia pinnata* 'Superba,' with its sculptural, bronze-tinted leaves and sprays of rose-pink flowers. Make a feature out of a dark boundary wall by smothering it with a twining vine or ivy. A planting of hellebores or pots of summer annuals will add pockets of color to this green oasis.

There are, then, many ways to utilize shady areas to your advantage, but in some gardens the problem is how to create a retreat away from the constant glare of full sun. Walls and hedges will throw some welcome shade onto the garden, and a cool, shady spot under a spreading tree is a good place to relax in summer. Verandas, arbors, and pergolas make comfortable, sheltered areas for alfresco dining, or add a large outdoor parasol to evoke the atmosphere of a Mediterranean garden.

Ferns, hostas, and the pink heads of *Persicaria bistorta* 'Superba' surround a handsome pot to form an interesting composition of different shapes and textures in this shady border (right). These shaded York stone steps are lightened with pale plantings of lavatera, *Alchemilla mollis*, and the rambling *Rosa* 'Bobbie James.' Terracotta pots planted with cream tobacco plants (*Nicotiana*) inject additional splashes of light (opposite).

*"Nature will bear the closest
inspection. She invites us to lay our
eye level with her smallest leaf, and
take an insect view of its plain."*

H.D. THOREAU

pattern

NATURE OFFERS A CORNUCOPIA OF SHAPES and patterns to delight the eye
and lift the spirits: the delicate tracery of a bird's footprint on a fresh
covering of snow, the exquisite gossamerlike thread of a spider's web in
the early morning sun, or the alluring silhouette of distant trees at dusk.

In the same way that you use such things as furniture, wallpaper, and
fabrics to stamp your own personality on the rooms of your house, so
in the garden you can call upon plants, hardscaping, different color
combinations, and ornaments to decorate the space and introduce
interesting variations of pattern. In an informal cottage-style garden, there
will be masses of flowers in different colors, shapes, and sizes; in a more minimalist
setting, pattern will be created by architectural foliage plants, pebbles, rocks, and
perhaps a rectangular pond.

Whatever your preferred style of garden, always remember to incorporate plenty
of green into the plan – either as a feature in its own right in the form of an elegant
conifer, perhaps, or as a framework or foil for other plants. This is especially
important in a formal-style, garden where other colors may not play a significant role
and where evergreen topiary, hedges, parterres, paths, and edges predominate to
form a geometric pattern. Clipped hedges, whether planted on the perimeter or used
to divide the garden into different sections, help to cement the overall symmetry of
the pattern. An edging of low, clipped boxwood gives definition to a flowerbed, and
a serried line of formally pruned trees creates a distinct pattern along a driveway.

Before embarking on any new planting plan, it is useful to think about how pattern
is used on the wallpaper and fabrics in your home to create a harmonious effect.
Look at the way the pattern is repeated
several times and not just printed in a
haphazard way, and notice how the same
colors are continued throughout the
design. The same principles should be
applied to the garden. In a long bed, for

A sunken pond with square stepping stones and
plantings of blue iris, hostas, and grasses creates an
eye-catching formation of pattern (opposite). Close
inspection of plants such as *Osteospermum* 'Pink
Whirls' (above) or the dew-kissed leaf of an *Alchemilla
mollis* (right) will reveal exquisite details.

Nature offers a rich tapestry of different shapes and patterns (above). Here red and green lettuce form a decorative spiral while a living sculpture is formed from an arrangement of cacti. Foliage provides an exciting range of pattern, including the heavily veined bright green leaves of a cabbage, the serrated fingers of *Melianthus major*, and the sharp white spines of a cactus.

instance, a flow or drift of the same color will be more aesthetically pleasing than erratic blobs of color and odd shapes dotted here and there. Repeat plantings of the same species or color will also produce a pleasing pattern. Vegetable and herb gardens lend themselves well to this form of planting, with neat rows or blocks of the same species forming a pleasing arrangement. An espaliered fruit tree also makes a striking pattern on a wall.

Plants themselves offer a bounty of exquisite patterns and shapes. Ferns are prized for the diversity of their foliage, from the impressive umbrellas of *Dicksonia antarctica* to the feathery fronds of the lady fern *Athyrium filix-femina*. Consider, too, the toothed leaves of *Agave americana*, the swords of a yucca, the hands of a mahonia, the many-

The arching branches of *Liquidambar styraciflua* form a stunning blanket of pattern and color (above).

fingered leaves of the cardoon (*Cynara cardunculus*), and the feathers of love-in-a-mist (*Nigella damascena*). Euphorbias, hostas, grasses, and cacti are also noteworthy for their architectural foliage and make a splendid backdrop to other plants.

Flowering plants provide the gardener with a rich pool of pattern, from the perfect wheel of an osteospermum to the shy, nodding bells of lily of the valley and the charming waterside flowers of angel's fishing rods (*Dierama pulcherrimum*). The bottlebrushes of callistemon, the towering spires of delphinium, the fiery pokers of torch lily, the dangling hearts of bleeding heart (*Dicentra spectabilis*), and the prickly balls of sea holly – only nature could have created such perfect forms, and all add interest and dimension to the garden.

Trees are important for the shape and pattern of their leaves and for their wide variety of habits – tall and thin, round and bushy, or weeping. Some also produce superb bark that can help to bring welcome splashes of pattern and color to an otherwise dull winter garden. *Prunus serrula* is prized for its outstanding shiny, red-brown horizontal bands, the graceful *Betula utilis* var. *jacquemontii* offers a stunning display of pure white bark, and *Acer griseum* has a glowing mahogany trunk and peeling orange bark. The winter stems of dogwoods (*Cornus* species) – ranging from red and purple to gold and orange – look magical when planted in blocks, especially when they are teamed with the ghostly purplish white stems of *Rubus cockburnianus*. Many species of eucalyptus also have distinctive bark and make an unforgettable sight in a woodland setting.

You can also achieve interesting patterns with hardscaping. Paths, steps, and paved areas can all make arresting features in their own right, helping to divide the yard into separate compartments and introducing changes of level. Paths, beds, and even ponds can be used to create a symmetrical pattern or to introduce curves. Other sources of pattern could come from the intricate filigree of a wrought-iron gate, the rounded form of a stone statue, or the shadows cast by a boundary wall.

Each season brings its own individual gifts of pattern to the garden. A tapestried carpet of bulbs lights up the garden in spring, and in summer the sun's reflection darts and dances on a pool. The autumn garden is decorated with the plump, spherical shapes of pumpkins and squashes, and brilliant yellow, red, and orange berries hang like jewels from a firethorn. In winter the first frosts form a lacy pattern on evergreens, and bare branches droop under the weight of snow.

Spikes, tufts, and plumes abound in this ethereal winter border, where feathery grasses mingle with the sword-shaped leaves of New Zealand flax (*Phormium*), the russet heads of sedum 'Autumn Joy,' and the seed heads of asters (left). A naturalized clump of the red trumpet-shaped flowers of hippeastrum makes a stunning display against a backdrop of greenery (opposite).

part three

THE DETAILS

A GARDEN IS A PLACE TO BE ENJOYED, somewhere you can retreat to away from the cares of the world and where you can contemplate the changing seasons. There should be a seat or two so you can relax and watch the unfolding pageant of colors, shapes, and patterns. There might be a patio or paved area with tables and chairs where you can entertain friends, and a safe play area for children. Your garden should also be a haven for wildlife, so make sure there is a tree, a pond, a sweet-smelling shrub, or a birdbath. Creating a garden that is both functional and a pleasure to be in is all about paying close attention to the details – a path for easy access to different parts of the garden, a wall for privacy and shelter, a windowbox to cheer up the outside of the house, and a few ornaments to provide interesting focal points.

When planning a new garden, you should give as much thought to the structural features as you do to the planting plans. Decide what basic elements you need and tackle any construction work early. Perhaps you would like to lay a new lawn or add a garage, patio, storage shed, or even a swimming pool. Figure out where you would like paths, steps, a pond, or seats to go.

Think about the building materials you would like to incorporate – wood, stone, brick, gravel, concrete – and how they will harmonize with the house and garden. Local materials will

Stone has an inherent mellow beauty that lends itself well to water features such as this simple wall-mounted fountain trickling into an elegant pool.

add a vernacular charm to your property; they blend well with the surrounding landscape and are often inexpensive. Hard surfaces such as paving and decking also need to be practical and hard-wearing. Try not to have more than two or three different surfaces in the same area since this can be visually distracting. Safety is also of paramount importance, so call in a professional if you are thinking of adding a high boundary wall or a swimming pool.

Look carefully at the space to see how it can be improved. Can any existing features be adapted? You might be able to convert an old shed into a rustic eating area, for instance. If the garden is monotonously flat, build steps or a wall to introduce changes of level, or erect an arch or pergola to break up the space. You might want to add a hedge to camouflage an ugly view, or you could change the direction of a path to lead you to a more appealing outlook. Make sure the house and garden sit comfortably together. An intermediate structure such as a patio or a simple arch over the door can help to link the two.

Think seriously about investing in an outdoor lighting system in your yard. Having some artificial light will not only improve nighttime safety and security, it will also allow you to enjoy your garden for many more hours of the day.

Choose outdoor furniture, ornaments, and special features such as ponds or fountains that are in keeping with the style of the house and garden, and in scale with the surrounding landscape. Containers are an invaluable addition to any garden; even the smallest balcony can be transformed into a green oasis with a collection of pots spilling over with seasonal plantings.

Occasionally overlooked, sometimes inconspicuous, it is often the small details that can make such a difference to the overall comfort and harmony of the garden.

Whether grown in a conservatory or trained on a pergola or trellis, a scrambling grapevine makes a handsome living screen, helping to filter the sun's rays.

walls

A wall provides the perfect backdrop for a wide range of climbing plants, including this stunning *Clematis* 'Niobe' (above).

THERE ARE A NUMBER OF WAYS IN WHICH walls can be used to advantage in your garden. They help to define the boundaries of your property and provide privacy. They also afford a measure of shelter and protection for you and your plants. A brick or stone wall can be a decorative feature in its own right, or it can make an excellent backdrop for a range of climbing plants. Many rock plants, including campanulas, sempervivums, and saxifrages, look stunning when grown in the crevices of an old stone wall. Walls can also be used within the garden itself to mark off separate sections. Some places have restrictions on walls and fences, however, particularly those on the front and side boundaries of a property. In some areas, front walls are not permitted and most will have height or even material regulations. It is important, then, to check with your municipal authority before beginning any expensive construction work.

If you are building a wall on the perimeter of your garden, always check where the exact boundary lines lie. This will obviate any disagreements with neighbors in the future. You also need to consider how the wall will affect sun, shade, and light, not only in your garden, but also in neighboring gardens as well. This also applies to living walls, especially if you are considering planting a fast-growing tree such as the Leyland cypress (× *Cupressocyparis leylandii*).

If you have inherited a functional but unsightly wall, you can camouflage it with climbing evergreens such as ivy, or deciduous climbers such as a Virginia creeper (*Parthenocissus quinquefolia*), whose matte green leaves turn stunning shades of crimson in autumn, or *Vitis vinifera* 'Purpurea,' with rich purple autumn foliage. Other suitable species include roses, clematis, wisteria, *Actinidia kolomikta*, *Hydrangea petiolaris* and, for warmer climates, the prolific potato vine (*Solanum jasminoides*), with white and lilac-tinged blooms.

The most commonly used materials for walls are stone, brick, or concrete. All are suitable for use as boundaries – be they retaining, high, or low walls – but always choose the one that will sit most comfortably with the design of the house, the style of the garden, and the surrounding landscape. Retaining walls are designed to resist and hold back the earth behind them and to

An old lead container spilling over with colorful summer blooms thrives in this sunny corner (opposite). A weathered boundary wall is given a new look with painted trellis, a stately urn of bright red *Tulipa* 'Triumphator,' and a row of clipped topiary shapes planted in the gravel (below).

prevent the soil from sliding downhill. Because they have a structural purpose, they need to be more substantial than freestanding walls, and they are most useful on sloping sites. Whether retaining or freestanding, any wall over three feet tall should be constructed by a professional to make sure the thickness, depth of footings, and drainage are correct.

Dry stone walls have an inherent vernacular charm that will enhance the look of a garden, but they should not be much more than three feet tall, and they should slope inward slightly at the top for greater stability. Brick walls are durable and in the right setting – a town garden, for example – they can look charming, especially when the bricks have acquired a patina of age. For a modern property, a concrete wall might be the ideal choice. Concrete blocks come in a range of colors and finishes, from smooth to coarse, and vary in weight and density. You can always enliven a dull concrete wall with a coat of paint. Choose neutrals that will blend in with the surrounding landscape or inject a note of subtropical vibrancy with shades of terra-cotta or pink. Reconstituted stone blocks are, in effect, concrete blocks faced with stone dust. They are also available in a choice of colors and finishes and make an inexpensive alternative to natural stone.

The mellow tones of a sunny brick wall are picked up by the hanging pots and containers, while a terra-cotta cat balances precariously on top (right). A ceramic snake fountain is framed by a climbing *Hydrangea petiolaris* on this shady wall. A luxuriant planting of shade-tolerant hostas, hellebores, and forget-me-nots at the base completes the tranquil scene (opposite).

THE TRANQUIL GARDEN

arbors and pergolas

IN THE GARDENS OF ANCIENT ROME, pergolas were a common utilitarian structure. Built of rough local wood and supporting grapevines, they helped to shade the paths. These simple passageways, with climbing plants scrambling over the framework, have been used for centuries in hot countries, providing relief from the sun and helping to deflect the glare when making the transition from the house to the garden.

In addition to affording some protection, pergolas also make decorative garden features, whatever the climate. They give external structure to the garden and help to form a link between the house and garden. They also make an ideal spot for container-grown plants. Covered in a profusion of scented climbers, these romantic, secluded havens are perfect places to sit and relax or even enjoy a shady stroll.

Pergolas add instant height to the garden and allow you to have some privacy. They often adjoin the house, but they can also be situated within the garden itself, where they make attractive focal points and can help to break up a flat, uninteresting space. A pergola built on the boundary of your property may also help to screen an eyesore or unwanted view.

Usually double-sided and letting in light at the top, the basic construction of a pergola can be adapted to suit any size or style of garden. Sometimes the piers, or supports, are made from brick or stone to match the house, but more commonly the framework consists of wooden posts and open, overhead beams. Trellis is often used to fill in the sides and on the roof. Another variation on the theme is a series of metal or wooden posts or arches joined with rails of chain or rope. This type of

"Coming to kiss her lips (such grace I found)
Meseemed I smelt a garden of sweet flowers:
That dainty odours from them throw around
For damzels fit to deck their lovers bowers."

EDMUND SPENSER

Who could resist walking through this romantic pergola, bedecked with *Viola cornuta*, *Rosa* 'Madame Knorr,' sprawling nepeta, and blue delphiniums?

Even the smallest garden can be enhanced by a vertical structure. In this potager (above), a simple trellis pyramid supporting sweet peas (*Lathyrus odoratus*) and pole beans rises above a bed of ornamental cabbages, rhubarb, and sunny marigolds.

structure is ideal for training roses since it allows plenty of light and air to circulate. Sometimes living archways are created when a species such as apple or pear trees, laburnum, wisteria, or grapevines are trained as cordons to form tunnels.

A one-sided structure that abuts the house or a boundary wall is usually known as a lean-to or an arcade. Usually higher and wider than a normal pergola and with a hard floor surface and a covered roof, this outdoor room is less exposed to the elements and makes a comfortable place for eating and entertaining.

When erecting a pergola, make sure the upright posts are firmly and securely embedded in the ground. The frame should be at least seven feet high on the underside to allow plenty of headroom, especially when long racemes of wisteria or bunches of grapes are hanging down in season. Don't let plants overwhelm the

This elegant pavilion blends harmoniously with the verdant landscape (above).

structure completely. One of the great joys of a pergola is the entrancing dappled light it throws on the ground, so thin out any climbers that threaten to obfuscate this. And remember, too, that much of the inherent beauty of a pergola lies in the simplicity of its form, so you should not detract from this by adding too many additional details. A wooden seat halfway down or at the far end should be enough to entice you to walk a little farther.

There are a host of climbing plants that can be successfully grown on a pergola, from the fragrant sweet pea (*Lathyrus odoratus*) to the magnificent racemes of wisteria or the bright yellow flowers of winter jasmine (*Jasminum nudiflorum*). Choose honeysuckle or the summer-flowering jasmine (*Jasminum officinale*) for their pretty flowers and delectable fragrance. In warmer climates, grow the trumpet vine (*Campsis*

radicans), with its exotic orange to red flowers, the heavily scented *Trachelospermum jasminoides*, and the prolific potato vine (*Solanum jasminoides*). The beautifully colored *Actinidia kolomikta* is ideal for clothing a pergola and, of course, there are rambler roses and clematis. For spectacular autumn color there is little to rival a Virginia creeper (*Parthenocissus quinquefolia*), and for a lush evergreen display consider one of the varieties of ivy with glossy, variegated foliage.

Another garden structure that has been around for many thousands of years is an arbor, or bower as it is sometimes known. Usually semienclosed and with space for a seat or bench, an arbor makes an enchanting shady retreat from where you can contemplate the garden in peace and comfort.

As with a pergola, the basic framework can be constructed from a variety of materials and can encompass a range of styles. Wood and trellis are commonly used, but ready-made wirework arbors are now very popular. An arbor usually has a solid

Shaded by a spreading elm tree, this Japanese-style hut with a seat in front commands a good view of the rectangular pool in this restful garden (below).

roof or is covered with sweetly scented climbing plants such as roses or honeysuckle. The sides can be open to let in more of the view, or they can be enclosed for more protection and to enhance the feeling of intimacy.

Always try to position your arbor so it faces an uplifting view or an attractive part of the garden – overlooking a pond or colorful flowerbed, for instance, or perhaps in a secluded grassy area, ideal for romantic picnics.

A simple metal arch, just wide enough for a seat and covered with climbers makes a feature of a boundary wall or the side of the house, where it will provide wonderful dappled shade. This adaptable structure can also inject life into a forgotten corner of the garden. A shady nook can be incorporated into a high, thick hedge. Create a gap just wide enough for a seat or a bench, leaving a thin layer of hedge behind to act as a backdrop. Topiary arbors trained from yew make a stunning feature, but you can achieve a similar effect in much less time by covering a frame with fast-growing ivy.

This timber structure has open sides and trellis at the back to allow air to circulate on hot summer days (below), while a simple rustic arch with climbing roses and ivy scrambling up the supports adds height to this suburban garden (below right).

statuary and topiary

NO GARDEN WOULD BE COMPLETE WITHOUT some form of ornament, be it a man-made structure such as a stone statue or a living sculpture in the form of topiary. From the whimsical to the classical, from the abstract to the functional, statuary is a very personal matter and should reflect your own individual tastes. Whether you choose a large earthenware pot, an urn, an armillary sphere, or an obelisk, or opt for an abstract piece set on a plinth or a pair of resin sheep sitting quietly under a tree, there is something to suit every style and size of garden. A statue will provide interest throughout the year and can often look most dramatic set against a winter landscape. Scour junk yards and flea markets for interesting, original pieces, such as stone pineapples, finials, columns, vases, and urns, or look for good modern reproductions made from reconstituted stone.

In addition to their aesthetic qualities, ornaments also serve a number of useful functions. They add vertical height to a flat area and give internal structure to the garden. Often used as focal points at the end of a vista, they draw the eye to a

particular part of the yard and can help to indicate which way to proceed, either physically or visually. A large urn mounted on a matching pedestal at a corner of the garden acts like an arrow showing you which way to turn. Similarly, a pair of obelisks, urns, or topiary sculptures at the head of a flight of steps will help to lead you down, or placed at the bottom they encourage you to keep going up. A matching pair of ornaments is also a handsome way to frame another focal point, making an entrance for you to walk between.

Topiary hens and chickens are at home on the lawn (above).

This sculpture of a woodland sylph by Evert den Hartogh rises seductively above the giant leaves of *Petasites* (opposite).

Sculptures do not always have to be set apart from the rest of the garden and viewed from a distance to create a dramatic impact. In a wild garden or a woodland setting, it can be wonderful to happen upon an unexpected statue – a small figure of Pan, say, peeping out from lush, green foliage – at one with its natural setting. The main point to bear in mind when choosing a piece of sculpture is that it should be in scale and harmony with its surroundings. Choose mellow colors where possible and remember that having too many points of interest can be distracting. A garden that is crammed with statues will begin to resemble a graveyard, so limit yourself to one or two well-chosen, sympathetically positioned pieces.

For centuries, water and sculpture have been inextricably linked. No Japanese garden would be complete without these two elements, and many of the great gardens of the world, such as Versailles in France, boast spectacular water features.

An ornate ceramic fountain set in a pool with complementary edging creates an eye-catching focal point in a formal garden (right). The shape of the pool is echoed in the boxwood hedging behind.

Even the tiniest of gardens can accommodate a wall-mounted fountain with water trickling onto stones, or perhaps a small birdbath. Larger, more traditional statues or strong, modern pieces look best in a more open setting, whether at the edge of a lake or in the center of a good-sized pond.

Creating living sculptures requires patience and imagination in equal measure, but the results can be as beautiful as they are individual. Large or small, topiary statues always make an exciting focal point and add a theatrical touch to any garden. You can clip small-leaved shrubs – usually box or yew – into a galaxy of weird and wonderful shapes: from geometric spheres, pyramids, and spirals to peacocks, dinosaurs, top hats, even a complete chess set. Grow smaller specimens in pots so they can easily be moved around the garden and look for ready-made wire frames that can be covered quickly with fast-growing ivy.

This handsome wall-mounted birdhouse nestles in a quiet corner of the garden among a planting of foxgloves and white climbing roses (right).

lighting

THE WONDERFUL THING ABOUT HAVING SOME FORM OF lighting in your yard is that
it will greatly increase the number of hours you will be able to spend outdoors,
enabling you to enjoy your garden – for work or play, dining or relaxation – even
when darkness falls. A few well-placed spotlights or some candles at a patio table
will enhance the ambience of your garden, making it a pleasure to be in at all times
of the day. A garden that is lit up at night will also seem less cut off from the rest of
the house and will look wonderful from an upstairs window even when it is too cold
to venture outside. You can also use lighting to dramatic effect to make a stunning
nighttime feature of a statue or perhaps a handsome shrub or tree. Moreover, having
some form of illumination above an outside door, say, or around such things as paths,
steps, or a pool will bring additional safety and security to your garden.

If you are planning a new garden, think carefully about your lighting requirements
and try to complete any necessary installation work sooner rather than later to avoid
any potentially costly and disruptive changes in the future. The system can be as
sophisticated or as simple as you wish, but remember that safety is the key. Always
enlist the services of a qualified electrician. Powerful artificial light usually needs to

Decorative and
functional, these
spotlights shining up
through the gravel help
to define the edge of
the path (opposite),
while a strategically
positioned downlight
bathes a contemplative
stone Buddha statue
in light (left).

be wired from the house, with cables and wires buried to a specific depth. Less-expensive, low-voltage systems can be plugged into an exterior socket, but cables will usually be exposed and you will need to be careful when mowing or weeding. The advantage of this system, however, is that lights can be moved around easily to accentuate different features at different times of the year.

Patios, verandas, terraces, and balconies will probably need to be bathed in the most light. Where these areas abut the house, the lighting system can be run easily from the inside. Freestanding, overhead, or wall-mounted lights can all be used to provide illumination for comfortable outdoor living, but always try to choose a style that is in harmony with both the house and garden. An elegant antique lamp would look wonderful on the veranda of a country house, while in a modern town garden a contemporary style would be more appropriate. It is also a good idea to make sure the lights can be switched on or off from both inside and outside.

Elsewhere, it is the contrast between areas of light and darkness that makes the garden at night such an atmospheric and magical place. The best advice is to keep it simple. Your aim should not be to flood every square inch in glaring light, but to illuminate points of interest and introduce subtle variations of light. There are a

Natural and artificial light join forces to produce interesting contrasts of illumination in this magical water garden (below).

number of ways that light can be channeled in the garden, so it is important to choose the right system for the task. Spotlighting, for instance, is sharp and will focus on a small, confined area; therefore it is ideal for picking out a stunning feature such as an ornament or an attractive plant. Spotlights should be positioned so they won't dazzle the eyes and don't shine directly into a neighbor's yard. By contrast, floodlighting produces a diffused light and is useful for illuminating a larger area of the garden.

Uplighting from below helps to create wonderful shadows and silhouettes in the garden, especially when it is positioned under a tree. The bare branches will be shown off to stunning effect in winter. Wall-mounted downlights throw light down onto a specific area or group of plants. They can also be used to focus on paths, steps, gates, and doorways. For further variation and to accentuate features such as striking foliage or bark, try lighting from the back or side. This will throw the plant into relief and create intriguing patterns and silhouettes. Whatever system you choose for your garden, remember that white light is usually more effective than colored light. Make sure you have the right bulb for the job and try to make the light fixture as unobtrusive as possible.

A dramatic nighttime mood is set in this garden, where clever accents of light are used to highlight the wooden bridge and the cascading waterfalls in the background (below).

Even the most subtle injection of light can be enough to enhance the overall atmoshere of a garden and prolong the hours of pleasure. Simple candles, an amber bottle reflecting in a wall, and thin, vertical glass tubes of light all help to create an ambient evening mood (opposite).

"'Yes,' I answered you last night;
'No,' this morning, sir, I say.
Colours seen by candle-light
Will not look the same by day."

ELIZABETH BARRETT BROWNING

Pools and water features are worthy candidates for some subtle nighttime illumination. In warmer climates, lighting will enable you to enjoy an outdoor swimming pool when the sun has gone down. Even in the smallest yard, a fountain will look magical when it is lit from above or below. Again, safety is the watchword. Water and electricity can be a dangerous combination, and the lighting system should be installed by a licensed expert when the pool or pond is being constructed. For the best results, try to make sure that the light source is concealed and keep the water as clean as possible as the light will quickly show up any dirt or algae.

Many sources of light do not require electricity or wiring. Candles and hurricane lamps will enhance the ambience and intimacy of the garden at night, and a bowl of floating candles makes a stunning centerpiece for an outdoor table.

Globes of light cast a mellow glow over a planting of grasses and golden achilleas (left).

"The hawthorn bush, with seats beneath the shade,
For talking age and whispering lovers made."

OLIVER GOLDSMITH

furniture

NO TRULY TRANQUIL GARDEN WOULD BE COMPLETE without a few pieces of furniture, even if it is no more than a couple of foldaway chairs that allow you to relax and enjoy the garden in summer. As more people than ever before are now catching the gardening bug, so the demand for comfortable, hardwearing outdoor furniture that is both functional and attractive to look at continues to increase.

Garden centers and catalogs now offer an almost overwhelming choice of styles to choose from, but before you rush out to buy the latest design, take time to assess your requirements. Do you like to sit out in the yard every day and for as many months of the year as possible, or is it a luxury that usually happens only on weekends? Would you like to eat or entertain outdoors on a regular basis?

It is important that the furniture you choose is in keeping with the style of the house and garden, and is the right size and proportion for the setting. Just as a sofa can enhance the look of your living room, so a garden seat or table should match the mood and ambience of the setting. Pretty wrought-iron café tables and chairs look wonderful in a Mediterranean-style garden, but they would strike a slightly discordant note in a pared-down Japanese garden. Similarly, a pair of modern white plastic sun loungers might look rather conspicuous in a country-cottage setting.

You should also spare a thought for storage before you invest in any bulky pieces of furniture. Is there room indoors or a garage or shed where you can store items for protection and safety when they are not in use? Collapsible, lightweight pieces will

White furniture can be used to stunning effect against a green background. Here dainty Parisian chairs take center stage in front of a classical vase (opposite). A white seat brings a splash of light to this green setting (right) and is the ideal place to enjoy the evening scent of *Hesperis matronalis* 'Alba.'

save space and will be easier to move around. You should also consider one or two all-weather items that can happily be left outside all year-round.

Furniture that is going to be used regularly and for any period of time – for relaxing, dining, even working – also needs to be comfortable. If a seat serves a primarily decorative function or is only used occasionally – a wooden seat at the far end of the garden or an antique stone bench at the far end of a vista – then a few portable pillows will encourage you to linger longer.

For relaxed outdoor living, with at least some protection from the elements, patios, verandas, and pergolas are the ideal choice, and with the right they furniture can be turned into functional and appealing exterior living or dining rooms. If seats, tables, and chairs are to be left outside permanently, try to make sure they are sheltered from the wind and glaring sun, and ideally facing an attractive part of the yard. You should also apply a protective coating of an appropriate paint or varnish to wooden or iron pieces; this will not only prolong their life, but will also enhance their appearance. In cold climates, where damp and moss may be a problem, try to avoid siting permanent furniture under a large, dense tree.

While styles have continued to come and go according to fashion and whim, many of the early designs, made from materials such as stone, wood, and iron, have stood the test of time and are as popular today as ever. Traditional stone benches and seats look charming in a variety of settings, and you can now buy affordable reproductions made from reconstituted stone. A simple seat constructed from railroad ties set on old brick or stone piers is ideal in a country or woodland setting.

Wrought- and cast-iron furniture was widely used in the second half of the 19th century and add a touch of romance and nostalgia to the garden. Aluminum reproductions are lighter in weight and less expensive. Cane and wickerwork furniture is also evocative of another era, and although it can't be left outdoors it is relatively light and easily moved.

An evergreen hedge at the back and plantings of nepeta and honesty at the sides provide privacy and protection for this painted garden seat (opposite).

Dine outside in style at this elegant glass-topped table (below), or enjoy a few relaxing moments on a swing seat made of white ash (below center). A beautiful mosaic table and verdigris wrought-iron chairs occupy a tranquil part of the garden in front of a brick wall (below right).

This striking wheelbarrow makes a decorative addition
to the vegetable garden (above).

Teak is one of the most popular woods for ou̇door furniture and is used in many
designs – from simple director's chairs to elegant recliners, and from a simple picnic
table and bench to the most sophisticated dining table and chairs.

Furniture with a vernacular, rustic feel, made perhaps from local timber, looks
at home in a natural or wild garden, where more formal designs would seem out
of place. Conjuring up the romance of a medieval garden, grass seats – made from
thyme, chamomile, or simply well-clipped grass – are once again growing in
popularity. They can be freestanding or built against a wall or around a tree.
Wooden tree seats are also often seen encircling a large old specimen in a country
garden, and as well as being decorative to look at, they also provide a peaceful,
shady place to sit in summer. They are now available in easy-to-assemble kit form.

A shade of some sort – whether it is a small parasol for a table for two or a large
umbrella or canvas canopy that will shelter a party of twenty – is indispensable for
relaxed, comfortable alfresco dining. Your shade should be attached to a solid base
so it doesn't blow down with the first puff of wind, and it should be easy to
dismantle when it is not in use.

For the perfect finishing touch, why not have a hammock swinging gently on the
terrace or between two old fruit trees?

An unusual rustic seat picks out the colors of the
window frames and the blue ceramic pot (right), while
dining furniture has been chosen to complement the
trellis, archway, and plantings in this romantic paved
courtyard (opposite).

Take time to sit and enjoy the sights, sounds, and scents of your garden. This white wooden seat is perfectly positioned on the edge of an immaculate lawn and backed by roses, nicotiana, boxwood spheres, and the huge sword-shaped leaves of New Zealand flax (*Phormium tenax*).

containers

No GARDEN IS TOO SMALL FOR ONE OR TWO container-grown plants. Whether they are a temporary decorative addition or a permanent fixture, pots, windowboxes, hanging baskets, and tubs allow you to indulge in creative and flexible gardening on a small scale and will repay even the most inexperienced newcomer to gardening with a colorful seasonal display.

There is a huge array of containers to suit every taste and budget. Materials range from terra-cotta, stone, and wood to concrete, plastic, and galvanized steel. Terra-cotta has been an integral feature of gardens for centuries, and it has an earthy, natural appeal that looks appropriate in a wide variety of settings. Choices include large and small troughs, windowboxes, pots of every size, and huge oil jars – which often look most dramatic when they are left unplanted. Old chimney tops can also be commandeered into service and look effective when they are planted with trailing geraniums, lobelia, *Convolvulus sabatius*, or nasturtiums.

Stone troughs, boxes, urns, and vases have always been popular, and now with the introduction of reconstituted stone they are much less expensive. An old, slightly battered stone urn always adds a touch of romance to any setting, but you can speed up the weathering process by painting an occasional coat of milk or yogurt onto a new container to encourage the growth of lichen and algae.

The half-barrel or wooden tub are also stalwarts of the container garden. They are ideal for planting larger species, and if they are treated inside and out with a

An old kitchen sink planted with irises and rushes has been transformed into a miniature water garden (right). A terra-cotta flowerpot man makes a charming wall sculpture (left).

nontoxic preservative, they can remain outdoors even in cold climates. A barrel that has been properly sealed can even be transformed into a charming water feature with the addition of a few miniature water lilies.

Planters are another versatile option. Wooden models or the elegant Versailles planter are ideal for roof gardens or an area where weight is an important consideration. Old lead cisterns, watering cans, or ceramic sinks can all make useful planters and look most effective when combined in a group setting. Where space is at a premium, windowboxes and hanging baskets are the ideal choice. They help to dress the outside of the house and are a boon for people living in the city. Wall-mounted containers spilling over with trailing plants are also effective in a small space such as a patio or courtyard.

As with any other area of gardening, a level of maintenance is required to keep your plants in top condition. Containers dry out quickly in summer, so make sure your plants are kept well watered. Hanging baskets in particular will require a good daily soaking in the summer months. All pots need holes in the base, and you should cover these with pottery shards or pebbles to facilitate good drainage. Mount large containers on bricks to keep them off the ground and make sure the water drains away. Choose an appropriate potting medium and weed, deadhead, and control pests regularly. Your pots should also be heavy enough not to blow over, and they should be the right size for the plant. Wall-mounted containers and baskets must be securely fastened, and windowboxes must sit firmly on the sill so they don't topple off. Always check that the pot is weather-resistant and can be left outside all year-round; unglazed clay or terra-cotta, for instance, will dry out quickly in hot climates and will crack in cold winter climates.

Against a backdrop of sparkling *Lavatera* 'Barnsley,' this empty Cretan urn and ram's head sculpture create a theatrical display (opposite). A pale blue ceramic container is a perfect foil for the purple violas (above), while the mellow tones of a large terra-cotta pot complement the stunning topiary peacock (right).

The great beauty of containers is that you can try almost anything – from colorful annuals and aromatic herbs to miniature trees or even exotics that would not survive in other areas of the garden – and you can move them around or transfer them indoors if necessary. Containers can be used as a single eye-catching focal point or can be massed together. They inject instant height, structure, and color, and can be used in the main garden or on patios, balconies,

roof gardens, courtyards, or windowsills. Containers can enliven a dreary corner and give instant color to a damp, shady area where nothing else will grow. They can even be positioned to screen an unsightly object such as a drain, and because they are portable, you will be able to take them with you if you move.

In larger gardens, a few strategically placed pots can help to give a sense of direction and improve the overall balance of the space. Containers sit comfortably at the base of columns or the piers of a pergola and make wonderful focal points at the end of a path or vista. Placed on each side of an entrance door, a gate, or even a flight of steps, a pair of matching pots planted with enticingly scented plants will encourage you to go forward.

Herbs such as thyme, mint, and rosemary are ideal for growing in containers; position them near the door so they can be easily picked and to allow their delicious scent to waft into the house as you brush past them. Some vegetables also do well in pots and can offer a decorative display as well as an edible harvest. A willow spiral looks magnificent with scarlet runner beans trained over it.

Grouping pots of similar shape and size can look very effective. Here old-fashioned rhubarb pots planted with box impose a sense of order and balance on this herb garden (above). A row of terra-cotta pots planted with the golden yellow flowers of *Helianthus* 'Pacino' will enliven even the smallest space (above left).

There are many shrubs and trees that thrive in pots. For an instant Mediterranean look, plant lavender or citrus fruits, such as oranges, lemons, and kumquats or in large terra-cotta pots. There is also an old theory that figs produce a more prolific and better quality crop in a container where their roots are contained. Bay and olive trees make handsome specimens, and there are now many dwarf selections of fruit trees, such as pears and apples, that will yield a reliable harvest when grown in a container. You can also grow strawberries in a pot or even a hanging basket.

Pots of clipped box topiary and small evergreens make eye-catching focal points, or they can be used to form the backbone of a colorful seasonal display. They are a good way to introduce interesting shapes and different heights into the garden, and as evergreens they create interest all year-round. They look particularly enchanting in winter when they are dusted with a layer of snow.

Roses have a compact root system that makes them easy to cultivate in pots, particularly the smaller cultivars. The romantic weeping and standard types also do well, but remember that roses must never be allowed to dry out completely.

Tall galvanized buckets that hold pink roses look striking massed together (above).

Framed by the warm yellow of a climbing *Rosa banksiae* 'Lutea,' this welcoming front entrance is enhanced by an assortment of pots planted with white geraniums, red tulips, and osteospermums.

grass

AN AREA OF VERDANT GRASS IS ONE OF the most restful and versatile features of a garden. Whether it is roughly mown or immaculately manicured, grass has an intrinsic softness that will enhance any garden and provides a pleasing foil for the shape, texture, and color of other plants.

Lawns make attractive features in their own right, and they also help to give definition to flowerbeds. Gentle curves will add visual interest and informality to a larger garden, while geometric shapes such as a rectangle or a hexagon are more appropriate for a formal garden. In a small, square garden, a circular lawn will soften the angularity of the space and make it appear larger.

The quickest way to create a new lawn is to lay sod. Sowing seed is a less-expensive method but takes longer to establish. For an ornamental lawn, you could consider the low-growing and fragrant chamomile (*Chamaemelum nobile* 'Treneague') as an alternative to grass.

Lawns do best in an open, sunny spot. They need plenty of water in summer and adequate drainage to prevent them from becoming waterlogged in winter. In smaller gardens, where a lawn is often the main focus of attention, the grass must be well maintained and kept in good condition. A dried-out brown lawn filled with weeds will do little to refresh the spirits, so make sure the grass is well watered and weeds are kept under strict control. You will also need to make sure any leaves are regularly raked. There should be easy access for mowing, and edges should be neatly clipped off, especially if they abut a bed or path. Stepping stones of brick, wood, or stone make an attractive path across a lawn and help to reduce wear and tear in heavy-traffic areas. You can also combine grass and paving to form a distinct pattern.

In larger gardens, an area of roughly mown grass will help to create a gentle transition between the edge of a formal lawn and the natural landscape beyond the garden's boundary. A large lawn also looks wonderful when it is mown in strips to create a distinct pattern. In old country gardens, there are often meandering grassy paths. These are perfect in areas such as an orchard, a woodland, or a wildflower garden, where a hard surface would detract from the natural beauty of the setting.

"Breathless, we flung us on the windy hill,
Laughed in the sun, and kissed the lovely grass."
RUPERT BROOKE

A carpet of lush green grass leads down to the water's edge in this natural setting.

gravel

AVAILABLE IN A CHOICE OF COLORS AND IN various particle size, gravel is widely used to cover large areas of the yard such as driveways and paths. Inexpensive and quick and easy to lay, this versatile material provides an unobtrusive and neutral background and is easy on the eye and underfoot. It flows naturally around corners and bends and adapts well to awkward shapes. Gravel has been used as a hard surface for thousands of years – in Japan it is raked to form symbolic patterns – and it looks equally at home in an old-fashioned country garden, a formal garden, or in a modern setting where it is often used to create an illusion of water.

Gravel blends well with other hard and soft materials, and it has long been prized for its decorative qualities. It is an integral component of knot gardens and parterres, where it is used not only as paving to give definition to the geometric pattern created by dwarf box, but also to fill in the center of the beds. Gravel is a traditional feature of herb and rose gardens, and it makes a splendid foil for a topiary sculpture or a specimen tree. Steps look wonderfully rustic when railroad ties are used as the risers and gravel for the treads. Gravel can also be combined with other paving materials to create interesting variations of texture.

There are a number of species – including thyme, marjoram, lady's mantle (*Alchemilla mollis*), foxgloves, verbascum, and azaleas – that will happily thrive planted in gravel, and it is perfectly possible to create an entire garden using this medium.

A layer of gravel will also make a highly effective mulch, helping plants to conserve moisture in summer and facilitating surface water to run off.

Laying gravel on black plastic sheeting will help to keep paths and driveways free of weeds and other self-seeding plants. A curb of brick, wood, or stone on each side of a path will prevent loose chips from spilling over onto the lawn or flowerbeds.

Gravel is used to create a meandering dry stream, with larger stones and random clumps of plants defining the edges (opposite). Bricks and stepping stones are set into gravel to form a decorative path (left).

stone

OF ALL THE MATERIALS AVAILABLE TO THE GARDENER, stone is arguably the most aesthetically pleasing. Hardwearing and long-lasting, stone will add charm and character to almost any setting and can be incorporated into the garden in a myriad of ways – from grand terraces, steps, and paths to statues, urns, and fountains.

Use stone to conjure up the atmosphere of a Japanese or Mediterranean garden, or incorporate it into a more formal setting. A path or patio of cut stone with clipped grass in the joints looks modern and symmetrical, while roughly cut paving stones with gravel in the gaps has a rustic appeal. Dry stone walls have a vernacular charm that is appropriate for a country garden. Stone will enhance any water feature, be it the edge of a pool, a fountain, or even a cascading waterfall created from an outcrop of natural stone. Even utilitarian structures such as a barbecue or a bench can be transformed into decorative features when they are constructed from stone.

Natural stone is expensive to buy and transport, heavy to carry, and can be difficult to lay, but its beauty and durability repays the investment. Stone varies a great deal from one region to another, so it is always advisable to buy locally quarried stone, which usually will be less expensive and blend harmoniously with the natural landscape. Not all stone is frostproof, so you should make sure the stone you choose is suitable for your climate. This is particularly important for steps and paths, to make sure they do not become slippery and crack in winter's cold. It is also worth seeking old recycled stone that has already acquired a patina of age.

An old stone trough makes a charming planter for these white and purple pansies and golden tulips (below).

Dressed stone is trimmed to a regular shape and is easier to lay than natural stone. Random stone has an irregular shape and thickness that lends itself well to a more informal style of garden. It is easy to lay in curved areas and is ideal for crazy paving.

Reconstituted stone is a popular and affordable alternative to natural stone. Slabs of this material are widely used for paths and patios, and, being of uniform thickness, they are usually much easier to lay than natural stone. For a less monotonous effect, cut the slabs to different sizes or intersperse other materials such as brick or cobblestones.

A flight of moss-covered stone steps is surrounded by informal plantings of cool green ferns in this secluded garden (opposite).

Echoing the stone of
the house and wall, this
winding path leads to a
paved sitting area.

water

THERE IS A WATER FEATURE TO SUIT EVERY style and size of garden, from a natural-looking pond or elegant formal pool to a fountain or small wall-mounted spout with water gently trickling down over cobblestones.

Usually irregular in shape and blending imperceptibly with its surroundings, a natural pond will normally have its edges softened by waterside plants such as *Iris pseudacorus*, *Gunnera manicata*, *Butomus umbellatus*, *Primula florindae*, hostas, and the arum lily (*Zantedeschia*). For a more formal look, choose a rectangular or circular pond filled with romantic water lilies (*Nymphaea*) and with a decorative stone or tiled edge, or a rill set in clipped grass or gravel, reminiscent of formal Italian gardens.

Whatever style you choose, make sure your area of water is in scale and proportion to its surroundings. Too large and it can take over the whole space; too small and it can begin to resemble a dreary puddle.

A pond or pool requires a sunny, level position away from overhanging trees, whose falling leaves can damage the plants and wildlife. You should also try to site the pool in view of the house or create a special sitting area where you can enjoy the sights and sounds of the water.

You can buy ready-made pools in a choice of shapes, or you can construct your own by laying a large sheet of butyl rubber. Whichever option you choose, make sure there is a shelf for marginal plants. Black is the most successful color for pond linings because it acts as a mirror and increases the reflective quality of water. When your pond is in position, try to wait two weeks before adding plants, and then, ideally, another two weeks before introducing any fish.

A small garden or courtyard is the ideal setting for a simple splashing fountain, a water sculpture, a birdbath, or perhaps a small symmetrical pool set in wooden decking or stone paving and with a simple planting of yellow irises and interesting striped grasses. Even a simple container such as a sealed half-barrel can become an eye-catching water feature with the addition of a few miniature water lilies.

The calming properties of water can be incorporated into any size of garden. In this idyllic setting (right), a bridge made from Cotswold stone spans a cascading stream flanked by informal plantings. On a much smaller scale, a half-barrel has been transformed into a charming pool complete with a spouting bronze frog and surrounded by lush foliage (below).

wood

WOOD IS ONE OF THE OLDEST NATURAL materials known to man, and there is a place for it in practically every garden, whether it is for utility or decoration. Wood harmonizes well with other natural and man-made materials, and it can appear old and weathered or modern and sleek.

In many countries, wood is the main component of fences and gates, and it is also widely used for pergolas, arches, sheds, conservatories, and trellises. Available in a choice of beautiful shades and interesting grains, wood has a welcoming quality that lends itself well to outdoor furniture – from elaborate tables and chairs to modern deck chairs and chaises or a simple rustic bench made from old railroad ties or a weathered tree trunk.

Wood is popular for ornamental features such as bridges and sculptures, birdhouses and containers, and it is useful for edging garden beds and for supporting plants. Decking makes a wonderful forgiving surface for areas such as patios, terraces, and roof gardens, where its light weight and intrinsic softness give it the advantage over heavier materials such as brick or stone. Wooden stepping stones make a decorative feature over a lawn or across a pond or steam. You should think carefully before you use lumber for high-traffic, exposed areas of the yard such as paths and steps, however, as they can become dangerously slippery when wet.

There are two main types of wood: hardwood and softwood. Hardwoods, such as teak, oak, mahogany, and ash, come from broad-leaved deciduous trees. Teak is the most affordable and widely used hardwood for outdoor furniture. It is impervious to heat and water, and does not need to be treated, but it will fade and weather in time to a beautiful silvery gray. Softwoods, including fir, pine, and deal, are more affordable and easier to work with. Most are susceptible to rotting when left outside, however, and need to be treated with a preservative stain, varnish, or microporous paint.

Old wooden railroad ties set into gravel form a delightful, informal path (right). A wooden seat nestles under the branches of a spreading tree (left).

brick

EQUALLY AT HOME IN AN OLD COUNTRY COTTAGE garden or in a modern, minimal setting, brick is perhaps the most versatile and aesthetically pleasing man-made material for the garden. Brick blends well with other hard and soft surfaces such as stone, gravel, wood, or grass, and it provides a good backdrop for a host of plants.

Bricks can be used in a multitude of ways in the garden. They are widely used for walls and paths, and make excellent pavers for steps and patios. They provide a solid framework for gates, arches, and seats, and make an attractive permanent border for pools, raised beds, and even barbecues. Structures such as a boundary wall must be secure and built on firm foundations, so always call in a professional for any major construction work.

Bricks also vary in color, texture, and strength, and it is important to choose the right type for the job. For a paved area, for instance, you need to make sure the brick is hardwearing and weather resistant. You can buy specially made bricks that are tolerant of frost and capable of withstanding heavy wear and tear. The bricks must be firmly laid to avoid unevenness, and it is advisable to use mortar to prevent water

from soaking into the cracks and to stop weeds from peeking through. For an informal, little-used path, you can omit the mortar and allow plants such as violets or lady's mantle (*Alchemilla mollis*) to selfseed in the gaps. An algicide spray will help to counteract slippery moss and slime from forming on the surface, especially in damp, shady areas.

Bricks are relatively easy to cut, so they are ideal for creating circular or geometrical designs. The pattern or bond of your path or patio can be as simple or as intricate as you wish, but it is always a good idea to design it on paper first.

The mellow brick used for the wall and the archway is repeated in the patterned paved area (left). A terrace built from an eclectic assortment of bricks is softened by wandering foliage plants (right).

THE TRANQUIL GARDEN

sources

Antique Rose Emporium
9300 Lueckemeyer Road
Brenham, Texas 77833
T 409-836-9051 **F** 409-836-0928
Old garden roses, rose books.

Baker's Lawn Ornaments
Box 265
Somerset, Pennsylvania 15501
T 814-445-7028 **F** F 814-445-5462
Victorian gazing globes.

Kurt Bluemel, Inc.
2740 Greene Lane
Baldwin, Maryland 21013-9523
T 410-557-7229 **F** 410-557-9785
Ornamental grasses, sedges, rushes, bamboos, ferns.

Buena Creek Gardens
P.O. Box 2033
San Marcos, California 97079-2033
T 760-744-2810/8367 **F** 760-744-0510
Shrubs, vines, brugmansias, abutilons, salvias.

W. Atlee Burpee & Company
300 Park Avenue
Warminster, Pennsylvania 18974
T 800-888-1447 **F** 215-674-4170
Plants, seeds, books, supplies, tools, bulbs.

Completely Clematis
217 Argilla Road
Ipswich, Massachusetts 01938-2617
T 508-356-3197 **F** 508-356-3197
Clematis.

The Conard-Pyle Co.
372 Rose Hill Road
West Grove, Pennsylvania 19390
T 800-458-6550 **F** 610-869-7378
Modern hybrid roses and shrubs.

The Cooks Garden
P.O. Box 535
Londonderry, Vermont 05148
T 800-457-9703 **F** 800-457-9705
Seeds and supplies: vegetable and salad greens, edible flowers.

Copper Craft Lighting
5100-1B Clayton Road, Suite 291
Concord, California 94521
T 510-672-4337 **F** 510-672-4337
Landscape lighting.

The Cummins Garden
22 Robertsville Road
Marlboro, New Jersey 07746
T 732-536-2591
Rhododendrons, azaleas, dwarf conifers.

The Daffodil Mart
30 Irene Street
Torrington, Connecticut 06790
T 800-255-2852 **F** 800-420-2852
Spring-, summer- and fall-blooming bulbs.

Duncraft, Inc.
102 Fisherville Road
Penacook, New Hampshire 03303
T 603-224-0200 **F** 603-226-3735
Bird feeders, bird houses and accessories.

Fancy Fronds
P.O. Box 1090
Gold Bar, Washington 98251-1090
T/F 360-793-1472
Nothing but ferns.

Ferry-Morse Seeds
P.O. Box 488
Fulton, Kentucky 42041-0488
T 800-283-6400 **F** 800-283-2700
Bulbs, seeds, vegetables, perennials, supplies.

Forestfarm
990 Tetherow Road
Williams, Oregon 97544-9599
T 541-846-7269 **F** 541-846-6963
Western natives, unusual perennials, trees and shrubs.

FrenchWyres
P.O. Box 131655
Tyler, Texas 75713-1655
T 903-597-8322 **F** 903-597-9321
Wire garden accessories.

Gardener's Supply Company
128 Intervale Road
Burlington, Vermont 05401
T 800-863-1700 **F** 800-551-6712
Tools, supplies and home greenhouses.

Gardens Alive!
5100 Schenley Place
Lawrenceburg, Indiana 47025
T 812-537-8651 **F** 812-537-5108
Organic garden products.

Geraniaceae
122 Hillcrest Avenue
Kentfield, California 94904
T 415-461-4168 **F** 415-461-7209
Hardy and scented geraniums.

Glasshouse Works
P.O. Box 97, Church Street
Stewart, Ohio 45778-0097
T 800-837-2142 **F** 614-662-2120
Exotic and tropical plants.

The Gourmet Gardener
8650 College Boulevard
Overland Park, Kansas 66210
T 913-345-0490 **F** 913-451-2443
European herb, vegetable and edible flower seeds.

Greer Gardens
1280 Goodpasture Island Road
Eugene, Oregon 97401-1794
T 541-686-8266 **F** 541-686-0910
Rhododendrons, azaleas, vireyas and ornamental trees.

Gurney's Seed & Nursery Co.
110 Capital Street
Yankton, South Dakota 57079
T 605-665-1930 **F** 605-665-1671
Perennials, trees, shrubs, bulbs.

Heaths & Heathers
502 E. Haskill Hill Road
Shelton, Washington 98584
T/F 360-427-5318
Heathers and heaths.

Hedera Etc.
P.O. Box 461
Lionville, Pennsylvania 19353-0461
T 610-970-9175
Ivy cultivars.

Heronswood Nursery
7530 N.E. 288th Street
Kingston, Washington 98346-9502
T 360-297-4172 **F** 360-297-8321
Choice perennials and ornamental woody plants.

Jackson & Perkins Co.
2518 S. Pacific Highway
Medford, Oregon 97501
T 800-292-4769 **F** 800-242-0329
Roses, perennials and bulbs.

Johnny's Selected Seeds
Route 1, Box 2580
Foss Hill Road
Albion, Maine 04910-9731
T 207-437-9294 **F** 800-437-4290
Vegetable, herb and annual seeds.

Jung Quality Seeds
335 S. High Street
Randolph, Wisconsin 53957-0001
T 800-247-5864 **F** 800-692-5864
Seeds, plants, bulbs, supplies.

Kinsman Company, Inc.
Old Firehouse, River Road
Point Pleasant, Pennsylvania 18950
T 800-776-0575 **F** 215-297-0450
Garden tools and equipment.

Lilypons Water Gardens
P.O. Box 10, 6800 Lilypons Road
Buckeystown, Maryland 21717-0010
T 800-999-5459 **F** 301-874-2325
*Waterlilies, lotus, bog plants and
supplies.*

Logeee's Greenhouses
141 North Street
Danielson, Connecticut 06239
T 860-774-8038 **F** 860-774-9932
Greenhouse and tropical plants.

McClure & Zimmerman
P.O. Box 368, 108 W. Winnebago
Friesland, Wisconsin 53935
T 920-326-4220 **F** 800-692-5864
Spring bulbs and species bulbs.

Mellinger's, Inc.
2310 W. South Range Road
North Lima, Ohio 44452-9731
T 800-321-7444 **F** 330-549-3716
Seeds, plants and some 4,000 supplies.

**Grant E. Mitsch Novelty
Daffodils**
P.O. Box 218-CS
Hubbard, Oregon 97032
T 503-651-2742 **F** 503-651-2792
Daffodils.

Moon Mountain Wildflowers
P.O. Box 725
Carpinteria, California 93014
T 805-684-2565
Annual and perennial wildflowers.

**The Natural Gardening
Company**
217 San Anselmo Avenue
San Anselmo, California 94960
T 707-456-5060 **F** 707-766-9747
Imported tools, organic seedlings.

Niche Gardens
1111 Dawson Road
Chapel Hill, North Carolina 27516
T 919-967-0078 **F** 919-967-4026
*Native plants, perennials, ornamental
grasses, trees and shrubs.*

Nichols Garden Nursery
1190 North Pacific Highway
Albany, Oregon 97321-4580
T 541-928-9280 **F** 541-967-8406
Herbs and vegetables.

Park Seed Company
1 Parkton Avenue
Greenwood, South Carolina 29647
T 864-223-8555 **F** 864-941-4502
Plants, seeds, bulbs.

Peaceful Valley Farm Supply
P.O. Box 2209
Grass Valley, California 95945
T 530-272-4769 **F** 530-272-4794
Organic tools and supplies.

Plant Delights Nursery
9241 Sauls Road
Raleigh, North Carolina 27603
T 919-772-4794 **F** 919-662-0370
*Hostas, ornamental grasses, asarums,
heucheras and pulmonarias.*

Robinson Iron
P.O. Box 1119
Alexander City, Alabama 35010
T 256-329-8486 **F** 256-329-8960
Decorative ironwork.

Roslyn Nursery
211 Burrs Lane
Dix Hills, New York 11746
T 516-643-9347 **F** 516-427-0894
Plants for shady and woodland gardens.

John Scheepers, Inc.
23 Tulip Drive
Bantam, Connecticut 06750
T 860-567-0838 **F** 860-567-5323
Bulbs.

Seeds of Change
P.O. Box 15700
Santa Fe, New Mexico 87506-5700
T 888-762-7333 **F** 888-329-4762
Organically grown seeds.

Shepherd's Garden Seeds
30 Irene Street
Torrington, Connecticut 06790-6658
T 860-482-3638 **F** 860-482-0532
Vegetables, herbs, flowers.

Siebert & Rice
P.O. Box 365
Short Hills, New Jersey 07078
T 973-467-8266 **F** 973-379-2536
Italian terra cotta pots.

Siskiyou Rare Plant Nursery
2825 Cummings Road
Medford, Oregon 97501
T 541-772-6846 **F** 541-772-4917
Alpine and rock garden plants.

Smith & Hawken
P.O. Box 6900, 2 Arbor Lane
Florence, Kentucky 41022-6900
T 800-776-3336 **F** 606-727-1166
Garden tools and furniture.

**Southern Exposure Seed
Exchange**
P.O. Box 170
Earlysville, Virginia 22936
T 804-973-4703 **F** 804-973-8717
Heirloom herb and vegetable seeds.

Territorial Seed Co.
Cottage Grove, Oregon 97424
T 541-942-9547
*Sweet peas, sunflowers and other
annuals.*

Thompson & Morgan
P.O. Box 1308, 22 Farraday Avenue
Jackson, New Jersey 08527-0308
T 800-274-7333 **F** 908-363-9356
Wide selection of plants.

Tranquil Lake Nursery
45 River Street
Rehoboth, Massachusetts 02769-1395
T 508-252-4002 **F** 508-252-4740
Daylilies, Japanese and Siberian iris.

Trellis Structures
P.O. Box 380, 60 River Street
Beverly, Massachusetts 01915
T 978-921-1235 **F** 978-921-1110
*Traditional and contemporary wood
trellises.*

Van Bourgondien Bros.
245 Route 109, P.O. Box 1000
Babylon, New York 11702-9004
T 800-622-999 **F** 516-669-1228
Bulbs and perennials.

Andre Viette Farm & Nursery
P.O. Box 1109
State Route 608
Longmeadow Road
Fishersville,Virginia 22939
T 800-575-5538 **F** 540-943-0782
Broad selection of garden perennials.

Wayside Gardens
P.O. Box 1
Hodges, South Carolina 29695-0001
T 800-845-1124 **F** 800-457-9712
*Perennials, roses, ornamental trees
and shrubs.*

We-Du Nurseries
Route 5, Box 724
Marion, North Carolina 28752-9338
T 704-738-8131 **F** 704-738-8131
Rock garden and woodland plants.

White Flower Farm
P.O. Box 50, Route 63
Litchfield, Connecticut 06759-0050
T 800-411-6159 **F** 800-496-1418
Shrubs, perennials and bulbs.

Windrose Ltd.
1093 Mill Road
Pen Argyl, Pennsylvania 18072-9670
T 610-588-1037 **F** 610-599-0968
Unusual trees and shrubs.

Yucca Do Nursery
P.O. Box 104
Hempstead, Texas 77445
T 409-826-4580 **F** 409-826-0522
Plants from Texas and the Southwest.

index

acknowledgments

All photography © Clive Nichols except for pages **82–83** Eluned Price.

The photographer and publisher gratefully acknowledge the work and cooperation of the following:
t = top, b = bottom, l = left, m = middle, r = right

2–3, 9, 92–3, 174–5 The Old Rectory, Berks; **6** Mr and Mrs D Terry; **8** Harcourt Arboretum, Oxford; **10, 16, 163b** Keeyla Meadows; **15, 178** Preen Manor, Shropshire; **17, 68–9** Barnsley House, Glos.; **18, 84** Manoir aux Quat Saisons, Oxon.; **20t** *Daily Telegraph*, Chelsea '92; **20b** M Walker, Chelsea '94; **26–27** Chastleton Glebe, Oxon; **28** Stephen White; **29, 122** Dennis Fairweather; **32** Manor House, Walton-in-Gordano; **34–5** Janet Williams, H. Peschar Gallery; **36** Terence Conran, Chelsea '95; **37, 187** Roger Raiche; **38b** Naila Green; **40** Richard Coward; **41, 104** Suzanne Porter; **42, 50** Little Coopers, Hampshire; **44, 123, 127** Turn End Garden, Bucks; **46** Ephrussi de Rothschild, France; **47** Fiona Lawrenson; **48** Kim Wilkie; **49** Shaun Brosnan; **52** Pro Carton Garden, Chelsea '96; **54** Abbotswood, Glos.; **55** Julie Toll; **56, 60–1** J Dowle & K Ninomiya, Chelsea '95; **57** Tatton Park, Cheshire; **58** Woking BC, Chelsea '93; **62–3** Architectural Plants, Sussex; **64** Madison Cox, Chelsea '97; **66** F. Lawrenson & J. Simpson; **67** Bonita Bulaitis, Hampton Court '96; **71, 75t, 124b** Osler Road, Oxford; **74** Mill House, Sussex; **75b** Bassibones Farm, Bucks; **76** Saling Hall, Essex; **77** Exbury, Hampshire; **78, 103, 162** Jill Billington; **79** Myles Challis; **81l, 100, 101, 110, 159, 189** Wollerton Old Hall, Shropshire; **81r** LIttle Court, Crawley, Hants; **87, 102** Chenies Manor, Bucks; **95, 132** The Old Vicarage, Norfolk; **96** The Anchorage, Kent; **97r** John Simpson; **98** Pat Volk. H. Peschar Gallery; **99t** Lakemount, Cork, Eire; **99bl** The Cottage Herbery; **105** Old Rectory, Northamptonshire; **106** Lucy Gent; **107, 130bl** Huntingdon Botanical Gardens, US; **108–9** Herta Keller. H. Peschar Gallery; **111** Lucy Huntingdon, Chelsea '94; **112** Wolfson College Garden, Oxford; **113b** Hearns House, Oxfordshire; **116** Greystone Cottage, Oxon; **117** Elisabeth Woodhouse; **119** Coton Manor, Northamptonshire; **120, 164–5** Olivia Clarke; **124t** Mark Brown; **125** Myles Challis; **126, 160m, 170–1** Paula Rainey Crofts; **128** *Sunday Times*, Chelsea '94; **130tl** Cecily Hill House, Glos.; **134–5** Claus Scheinert; **138b, 139** Bourton House, Glos.; **140** Lucy Smith; **141** C. and Y. Bicknell; **142–3** Wendy Lauderdale; **144** Nigel Colborn; **145, 163t** Butterstream, Eire; **146l** Gordon White, Austin, Texas; **146–7** Geoff Whitten. Hampton Court '95; **147, 167** Roger Platts, Chelsea '96; **148** E. Den Hartogh. H. Peschar Gallery; **149** Henk Gerritsen; **150** Fiona Barratt; **151** Bunny Guinness, Chelsea 97; **153, 154, 155, 156br, 157** Garden & Security Lighting; **156bl, 169t** Emma Lush; **158** Anthony Noel; **160l** Christian Wright; **160r** Rachel Fletcher; **161** Tintinhull Gardens, Somerset; **168** Jeremy Lewick; **169b, 170l** Bunny Guinness, Chelsea '97; **171** Anthony Lockwood. Hampton Court '96; **176** Jane Fearnley-Whitingstall; **177** Denmans, Sussex; **178** Preen Manor, Shropshire; **180–1** Pam Schwert/S. Kreutzberger; **182** Stiffkey, Chelsea '94; **183** Christine Pritchard, Chelsea 97; **185** Lambeth Horticultural Society; **186** *Country Living*, Chelsea '93; **188** Eastgrove Cottage, Worcester.